The United Arab Emirates

From Desert to Universalism

The Epic of Modern Civilization

KEMAL YILDIZ

Dedication

**To His Highness Sheikh Mohamed bin Zayed Al Nahyan,
President of the United Arab Emirates and Ruler of Abu Dhabi,**

The emblem of wise leadership and visionary foresight, laid the foundations of renaissance and progress, transforming the UAE into a civilizational marvel that tells the story of an ancient people and a bountiful land. Through its sagacious vision, the UAE has become a global model of progress and excellence.

**To His Highness Sheikh Mohammed bin Rashid Al Maktoum,
Vice President of the UAE, Prime Minister, and Ruler of Dubai,**

An exceptional and inspiring leader, a symbol of dedication and creativity, a pioneer of the Renaissance, and a maker of glory. Under his prudent leadership, the UAE's miracle shines as a civilizational epic.

To the great leaders of the UAE,

Who weave from the desert sands a renaissance that touches the sky. Inspired by your wise leadership, the UAE has become a symbol of progress and prosperity.

To the enlightened minds,

Who illuminates the path of progress with knowledge and science.

To the believing hearts,

They see every new dawn as an opportunity to create new history.

And to all who believe that the UAE is not just a place, but an unending story of determination and a will that achieves the impossible.

KEMAL YILDIZ

Contents

Introduction

Amid the desert, where the golden sands narrate the chronicles of the time, a grand civilization emerged from adversity. This miracle of willpower and ambition manifested in the United Arab Emirates, transforming its desert sands into oases of creativity and innovation.

The book "UAE: From Desert to Global Civilization - An Epic of Modern Civilization" delves into this unique renaissance and narrates how this nation carved its name in glowing letters on the pages of history. The author takes us to the essence of the UAE's civilizational awakening, highlighting the importance of this transformation and what it represents as a model for remarkable civilizational development. He sheds light on the fundamental pillars upon which this renaissance was built, starting with the wise vision of the prudent leadership that made innovation and technology the foundation of their civilizational model.

The pages of this book reveal how this sandy land transformed into one of the most prominent modern civilizational centers on both local and global levels. The book unveils the secrets of this civilizational miracle, from the foundations that established this astonishing transformation to the creativity in building infrastructure and sustainable cities, culminating in the role of e-government and the wise leadership behind this civilizational awakening. The book will take us on an astonishing journey through the transformation of a nation from sands to luxurious towers, from caravans to airplanes. We will explore how the UAE has become an exemplar of progress and development amidst a region beset with diverse challenges.

We cannot comprehend the outstanding success of the UAE without considering the exemplary leadership model, which greatly contributed to turning vision into tangible reality. We cannot overlook the impact of this renaissance on the entire region, where it has become a hub for innovation and investment, inspiring ambitions and setting new standards for civilizational development.

This book is an invitation to discover the secrets of creativity behind this civilizational miracle and an unforgettable journey through an inspiring history of creativity. It reveals the secrets of the success of a nation that has managed to inspire the world with its aspirations and transformed from a traditional desert into a developed civilizational hub on the global stage, constituting an epic of civilization spoken of by generations.

This introduction is not just the beginning of a book but an invitation to an extraordinary journey that unveils the secret behind the UAE's transformation into an icon of progress and prosperity. It transports us to a world beyond imagination, where the desert wears a cloak of greenery, towers touch the sky, and dreams become reality.

KEMAL YILDIZ

Chapter 1

Wise Leadership in the United Arab Emirates

Wise Leadership and Its Impact on Stability and Growth

Wise leadership in the United Arab Emirates has been a crucial and primary factor in achieving stability and economic and social growth over the past decades. The impact of wise leadership in the UAE reflects a strong and ambitious strategic vision to build a prosperous and stable society. This vision forms the cornerstone of the UAE's success as a miracle of civilizational renaissance.

The leadership in the UAE is characterized by stability and balance, focusing on sustainable development and enhancing the economic and social well-being of both citizens and residents. The influence of wise leadership manifests in several important aspects

• Political stability: Wise leadership provides political stability and security in the UAE, enhancing the country's attractiveness as a hub for investment, business, and tourism.

• Economic development: The leadership's directives towards economic diversification, innovation, and entrepreneurship contribute to achieving diverse and sustainable economic growth in the UAE.

• Social welfare: The leadership prioritizes social welfare for citizens and residents by providing high-quality healthcare, education, and housing services.

• Human development: UAE leaders encourage the development of human resources, enhancing skills and talents through advanced education and training programs.

• Cultural diversity: Wise leadership promotes cultural diversity and respects Emirati people's diverse cultural heritage and traditions.

The impact of wise leadership on stability and growth in the UAE serves as a vital lesson in how vision and strategic planning can be used to achieve success and progress at both national and international levels.

UAE's Role in Regional Politics

The United Arab Emirates holds a distinguished position in regional politics and plays a vital role in promoting stability and development. The UAE's role in regional politics is a significant part of its civilizational renaissance, positioning the country as a key player in the Arab region and the Middle East. The UAE has been notable for its active role in fostering stability, international cooperation, and progress across various political and economic fields. Key aspects of the UAE's role in regional politics include:

• Mediation and Political Resolution: The UAE strives to promote peace and stability in the region through political and diplomatic mediation. For instance, the UAE has played a crucial role in Yemen and Libya, shifting the strategy from "military first" to "peace first".

• Regional Alliances: The UAE participates in regional and international alliances to enhance security and combat extremism and terrorism. An example of this is the UAE's involvement in the international coalition against ISIS and its support for stabilization efforts in Syria and Iraq.

• Economic Development and Regional Cooperation: The UAE works to strengthen economic and trade cooperation with regional countries, contributing to prosperity and sustainable development. Indicators also show a shift in the UAE's policy towards Iran, with the resumption of communications and the enhancement of trade and investment interactions.

• Cultural Diplomacy and Humanitarian Cooperation: The UAE encourages cultural dialogue and humanitarian cooperation with regional and international countries, promoting values of tolerance and peaceful coexistence.

• Active Role in International Organizations: The UAE plays an active role in international organizations such as the United Nations and the Organization for Economic Co-operation and Development, supporting humanitarian and developmental initiatives.

The UAE's role in regional politics reflects a wise and multi-dimensional diplomatic strategy aimed at achieving stability and development in the region, enhancing its image as a reliable international partner and a driving force for progress and regional cooperation.

UAE's Role in the International Community and International Organizations

The UAE's role in the international community and international organizations reflects an effective diplomatic vision aimed at enhancing international cooperation and constructive global interaction. The UAE is an active and committed player in international cooperation across various fields, from sustainable development to combating climate change and promoting international peace and security. The UAE's successful policy is based on peace and mutual respect, serving as a global model for tolerance and peaceful coexistence among diverse peoples. The UAE's contributions to global peace and sustainable development demonstrate a strong commitment to the values of international cooperation and building a more stable and prosperous world for all. The UAE is a leader in supporting peace and promoting sustainable development on a global scale, making tangible contributions in several areas. Key aspects of the UAE's role in the international community and international organizations include:

• Humanitarian and Development Aid: The UAE is one of the largest humanitarian donors in the world, providing financial and humanitarian aid to needy countries worldwide, whether for natural disaster relief or to promote sustainable development.

• International Cooperation in Health and Education: The UAE seeks to enhance international cooperation in health and education by launching innovative educational and health initiatives and programs in many countries.

• Participation in Humanitarian and Volunteer Work: The UAE encourages active participation in international humanitarian and volunteer work by sending medical teams and urgent aid to crisis areas. The UAE makes significant contributions to global humanitarian efforts, supporting the Central Emergency Response Fund and regional crisis relief, thus improving living conditions and supporting needy populations.

• Environmental Efforts and Climate Change Mitigation: The UAE is committed to environmental changes and combating climate change, promoting international cooperation in this field by hosting international conferences and summits on the environment. The UAE holds an influential position in humanitarian work and in addressing the impacts of climate change.

• Participation in International Organizations: The UAE plays an active role in international organizations such as the United Nations, the World Trade Organization, and the Gulf Cooperation Council. The UAE hosts the headquarters of many international organizations and institutions, reflecting its strength and status in the world, and strives to achieve common interests and enhance international cooperation.

• Political Settlement and International Mediation: The UAE is a key player in political settlement and international mediation to resolve conflicts and crises in the region and beyond. The UAE plays an active role in political settlements in Yemen and Libya and seeks to promote peace and stability in the region.

The UAE's role in the international community, international organizations, and global peace reflects a strong commitment to the values of cooperation and international understanding. It reflects a vision of a state striving to build a more stable and prosperous world for present and future generations.

The Impact of the UAE's Civilizational Renaissance on the Region and the World

The impact of the UAE's civilizational renaissance on the region and the world highlights the UAE's role as an influential cultural player both regionally and globally. This influence is evident in various aspects including the economy, politics, culture, and innovation. Some of these aspects are:

• Economy and Investments: The UAE is one of the most important economic centers in the region and the world, thanks to its diverse economy and focus on development and innovation. The UAE is a hub for foreign direct investment and provides a conducive environment for business and innovation, positively impacting the region and enhancing overall economic growth.

• Regional and International Cooperation: The UAE plays an active role in promoting regional and international cooperation across multiple fields, from trade to security, counter-terrorism, and climate change. This cooperation reflects the UAE's civilizational spirit and openness to the outside world.

• Culture and Heritage: Emirati culture and heritage serve as significant sources of inspiration and cultural interaction within the region and beyond. Promoting Emirati heritage enhances mutual understanding and cultural cooperation among peoples.

• Innovation and Technology: The UAE strives to enhance innovation and adopt technology in various fields, including renewable energy and digital technology. This pioneering spirit is evident in the

UAE and positively influences technological advancement in the region. The Dubai Expo 2020, which attracted visitors from all over the world and showcased the latest technologies and innovations, is a prime example.

• Sustainable Development and the Environment: The UAE is committed to promoting sustainable development and environmental protection, supporting international initiatives in this regard. This commitment has a positive impact on the region and the world by fostering environmental sustainability.

• Tolerance and Cultural Coexistence: The UAE is a model of cultural and religious coexistence, where people from different nationalities and religions live in peace and understanding. The UAE embraces values of tolerance and moderation and aims to promote this concept through programs and laws combating discrimination and hatred. International events such as the "Interfaith Summit" and the construction of the "Abrahamic Family House" have been organized to foster understanding among different religions.

The impact of the UAE's civilizational renaissance extends beyond the country itself to the region and the world. By enhancing education and culture, promoting tolerance and coexistence, developing the economy and innovation, and fostering stability, prosperity, and progress on regional and global levels, the UAE has become a civilizational force contributing to building a better future for humanity.

Chapter 2

The Historical Evolution of the UAE
From Past to Present

In the depths of history, the United Arab Emirates (UAE) shines as a rare gem on the Gulf coast, weaving the most splendid success stories and greatest achievements to form an epic historical tableau. It's a remarkable journey that extends from ancient times to the bright present, embodying rich heritage and continuous development, making it one of the most important nations globally and a distinctive tourist destination.

The UAE embodies an ancient civilization with roots deep in history, where diverse ancient artifacts and landmarks narrate a story brimming with trade, civilization, and cultural diversity. For thousands of years, the UAE has been a significant area on the world trade map, serving as a hub for commercial exchange between the East and the West. The UAE is closely linked with Islamic and ancient Arab civilization, flourishing with arts, sciences, and literature.

In the depths of Emirati history, we find traces of ancient civilizations harmonizing with the brilliance of diverse cultures. This region has been a center of trade and civilization since ancient times, hosting numerous artifacts that reflect its rich and diverse heritage, such as ancient cities, forts, towers, and religious temples. Al Ain, located in the Emirate of Abu Dhabi, stands out as one of the prominent archaeological sites in the UAE, with a history dating back thousands of years, underscoring the region's importance as a center of human life since ancient times.

The history of the UAE is characterized by depth and diversity, tracing back to ancient times when the land was home to nomadic groups relying on hunting and gathering. These groups emerged prominently in the

Stone Age, revealing a rich and diverse cultural heritage through archaeological excavations spanning ages from the Stone Age to the Iron Age.

In ancient times, the UAE stood out as an important commercial and economic center in the ancient world, strategically located to serve as a major station along ancient trade routes connecting the East and the West. Trade in pearls and maritime navigation were among the prominent economic activities in the UAE, with pearls being a crucial resource used by local populations for trade and livelihood. The UAE witnessed significant development in the pearl industry, making it a desirable hub for trade and cultural exchange. It received trade caravans from various parts of the world, contributing to the exchange of ideas and cultures among peoples.

The UAE has a coastline stretching along the Arabian Gulf, making it a vital location for fishing, pearling, and maritime trade. Fishing and pearl trading were essential sources of income and livelihood for ancient populations, leading simple lives relying on natural resources.

The UAE is renowned for its ancient archaeological sites, with findings dating back to the Stone Age in some archaeological locations. These artifacts reflect a rich history and cultural development that the region experienced over the ages.

During Islamic eras, the UAE thrived as an important commercial and cultural center along global trade routes. The UAE was significantly influenced by Islamic civilization, contributing to its economic and cultural growth. The importance of this period lies in trade and cultural exchange between the UAE and the rest of the Islamic world and other civilizations.

In Islamic times, the UAE was a key center of international trade, with coastal areas prominently serving as centers for commercial exchange with Eastern and Western countries. This was due to the UAE's strategic geographic location along maritime trade routes, making it a vital trading station on the route between India, China, the Islamic world, and Europe.

During this period, the UAE has witnessed significant cultural development, as many arts and diverse cultural practices emerged due to the blending of Islamic civilization with other cultures. This era saw the rise of artistic and literary schools, with Islamic architecture, decoration, and Arabic calligraphy flourishing as magnificent artistic expressions.

Today, the UAE presents a striking image of progress and leadership, with its modern cities and thriving economy. However, before reaching this high level of development, the UAE underwent a long journey filled with challenges and transformations throughout the ages.

Over time, the UAE experienced notable developments across various sectors, especially after the discovery of oil in the 1950s and 1960s. The discovery of oil attracted massive investments and contributed to transforming the UAE's economy from agriculture and fishing reliance to one primarily dependent on oil and gas.

Subsequently, with the UAE entering the modern era, its cities underwent immense transformations, embarking on the construction of advanced infrastructure and urban centers, making it one of the most developed countries globally.

Despite expanding horizons of development and progress, the UAE has maintained its heritage and culture, continuing to strike a balance between tradition and modernity. Through investments in cultural and heritage institutions and the organization of cultural events, the UAE reflects pride in its rich heritage and history.

The UAE has witnessed significant transformations, paving its way towards leadership and progress. Thanks to the wisdom and visionary leadership, the UAE transformed from a simple desert country to one of the most advanced and prosperous nations globally.

With the beginning of the 20th century, the UAE underwent a radical shift towards prosperity and development, with cities expanding and growing. Modern infrastructure saw remarkable development. In the modern era, the UAE witnessed massive economic and social resurgence, marking an important period in the country's history, achieving substantial progress in various fields.

With the establishment of the UAE federation in 1971, the UAE embarked on a new journey towards transformation and development. Efforts focused on developing infrastructure first, diversifying income sources, updating economic policies, and strengthening non-oil sectors like tourism, technology, education, and industry, aiming to enhance economic and sustainable development.

Through investments in education and human resource development, Emirati youth have been empowered to actively participate in the development process, fostering innovation and progress across various domains.

As the 21st century began, the UAE witnessed an unparalleled forward shift, transforming from a simple desert environment into one of the most advanced and diverse destinations globally. The UAE's vision for the future has been robust and ambitious, centered on infrastructure investment and enhancing economic and technological development.

The UAE government has embarked on ambitious development strategies aimed at raising the standard of living and improving the quality of life for both citizens and residents alike. In this context, the UAE has witnessed a significant increase in investment in sectors such as education, healthcare, tourism, and culture, with the goal of achieving sustainable development and enhancing economic diversification. The UAE has surpassed previous oil dependency and transformed into a global hub for diversity and comprehensive development. Thanks to wise leadership and ambitious development strategies adopted by the government, the UAE has witnessed an unprecedented cultural renaissance across various fields, making it one of the most prosperous and developed countries globally.

Behind this remarkable success lies the role of wise policies implemented by UAE leaders who mapped out the Renaissance and progress with foresight and wisdom. This vision was manifested through their understanding that true wealth does not solely rely on natural resources but lies in minds and knowledge, and investing smartly in key areas such as education, healthcare, and infrastructure. The UAE began wisely investing oil revenues by relying on natural resource returns to build the future, funding development projects and modern infrastructure. Since then, the UAE has continued its journey towards Renaissance and development with steady and confident steps.

The country has witnessed tremendous economic diversification and massive investments in various sectors. Investments were directed towards developing cities, improving public services, enhancing education, and fostering innovation, making it one of the most advanced and diverse countries globally. This has contributed to raising the standard of living and improving the quality of life for both citizens and residents alike.

Based on this wise vision, intensive efforts have also been directed towards enhancing education and innovation, with the establishment of leading educational institutions and the development of advanced educational programs. Innovation and entrepreneurship have been encouraged through the establishment of research centers and support for innovative projects. The UAE views education and innovation as fundamental to cultural renaissance and achieving progress and development, striving to enhance high-quality education and promote innovation in various fields.

Moreover, the UAE has made significant progress in education and human development, updating educational curricula, developing higher education programs, and providing exceptional educational opportunities, contributing to building a creative and educated generation that contributes to progress and innovation. The UAE adopts innovative educational policies aimed at stimulating creative thinking and developing innovation and critical thinking skills, including curriculum development that aligns with modern requirements and the integration of technology into the learning process.

The economy is also considered one of the prominent areas that have undergone radical transformations in the UAE in recent years. This is due to economic diversification strategies adopted by the government, leading to the development of industries, services, tourism, and technology sectors, making the UAE's economy more diverse, stable, and sustainable. The UAE began diversifying income sources and developing its various sectors. Significant government investments in infrastructure have created a conducive environment for attracting foreign direct investments, enabling the UAE to build a diverse and advanced economy based on various sectors such as energy, tourism, technology, education, and financial services.

The UAE is considered one of the countries that have wisely invested in economic diversification, understanding that directing the economy towards a variety of sectors enhances its resilience and stability. The UAE has started developing sectors such as tourism, technology, trade, and financial services, contributing to economic growth and job creation. Today, the UAE shines as an advanced player on the world map, becoming a key player in the global economy, competing internationally in areas of innovation, technology, and sustainability. Through hosting global exhibitions and international conferences, the UAE has affirmed its leading role in enhancing cultural, trade, and international cooperation exchanges.

In the cultural and social realm, the UAE has taken significant steps towards promoting tolerance, diversity, and human rights. Today, the UAE is home to more than 200 nationalities, making it a multicultural and multilingual society. Government efforts have included enhancing education and providing equal opportunities for all, contributing to the development of workforce skills and improving the standard of living.

Culture and art are integral parts of the Emirati identity, with artistic and architectural innovations evident in every corner of the UAE. The Burj Khalifa stands as a prominent example of stunning architecture, while the Palm Jumeirah represents an artistic masterpiece embodying the UAE's creative vision in transforming nature into a unique architectural landmark.

Furthermore, through the preservation and documentation of rich cultural heritage, the UAE contributes to enriching global culture and enhancing understanding among peoples. The UAE is also home to numerous museums and exhibitions preserving the region's cultural and historical heritage, allowing visitors to explore archaeological collections and exhibits that narrate the story of cultural evolution in the UAE.

The UAE offers diverse cultural programs and initiatives aimed at promoting cultural innovation. This includes organizing various cultural events such as art exhibitions, cultural shows, and creative workshops that foster cultural interaction and encourage creativity, aiming to build a learned and innovative society whose members possess critical and creative thinking skills and the ability to adapt to ongoing cultural and technological transformations.

The UAE recognizes the importance of education and cultural innovation as key drivers of cultural renaissance, striving to enhance high-quality education and promote innovation in various artistic and cultural fields. The UAE also focuses on developing creativity and innovation in literature, poetry, visual arts, music, and theater by supporting artists and providing opportunities for innovation and artistic expression.

In the field of environment and sustainable development, the UAE is globally recognized for sustainable development and environmental protection efforts, continuously working to preserve the environment and strike a balance between economic development and conservation of natural resources through the use of clean technology and diversification of energy sources. The UAE's vision reflects a strong commitment to sustainable develop-ment through a series of strategies and initiatives aimed at environmental conservation and sustainability across various sectors.

Moreover, the UAE promotes environmental awareness and encourages environmental initiatives within the community by organizing awareness campaigns and promoting the use of clean technology and sustainable environmental practices. The UAE government ensures strict environmental policies and laws to preserve the environment and combat pollution.

One of the key aspects of the UAE's efforts in sustainable development is the transition towards a green economy, where the UAE invests significantly in clean energy projects such as solar and wind energy. The goal is to increase the share of renewable energy usage to achieve environmental sustainability and reduce harmful emissions.

Given these concerted efforts, the UAE holds a prominent position in environmental protection and sustainable development, serving as a role model globally in sustainability and environmental conservation.

In the field of technology and innovation, the country has witnessed a significant leap in artificial intelligence, digital transformation, and advanced technological innovations, positioning it as a global hub for innovation and technology.

To achieve this cultural renaissance, the UAE has made substantial infrastructure developments by building world-class airports, an advanced network of roads, ports, and smart cities, contributing to boosting foreign investments and attracting global talent to the country.

The UAE is a leader in innovation and technology, with a focus on developing the tech sector and utilizing cutting-edge technologies in various fields. The strategic vision of the UAE is part of its efforts towards achieving sustainable development and transforming into a global hub for innovation and technology.

The significant investments by the UAE in digital infrastructure, through expanding internet networks, providing satellite communication services, and developing modern data centers, aim to create an enabling environment for startups and innovation. Additionally, establishing free zones for technology and innovation and providing support and funding for startup projects.

Furthermore, the UAE is adopting smart technology across various sectors such as healthcare, education, transportation, and energy, aiming to improve services, enhance efficiency, and enhance user experience. The government encourages innovation by launching competitions and initiatives that support innovative projects and foster initiative and creativity among young people and society at large.

Moreover, the UAE is home to global technological conferences and exhibitions, attracting many international companies and experts in the technology field to exchange experiences and ideas and learn about the latest developments in this field.

Furthermore, the UAE adopts an active foreign policy that seeks to enhance international cooperation and promote peace and stability in the region and the world.

Building on these comprehensive strategies and ambitious visions, the UAE continues to achieve successes and shine in the world of cultural renaissance and sustainable development. As a global center for diversity and advancement, the UAE continues to excel and lead in various fields, making it a role model for civilizational and economic advancement.

The journey of the UAE from simplicity to leadership embodies a story of admirable success, as it has succeeded in achieving comprehensive development and transforming its economy from oil dependence to a diverse and sustainable one. It has also built advanced infrastructure and developed sectors such as industry, education, health, and tourism exceptionally.

The wise vision of UAE leaders is the main driver behind its remarkable civilizational renaissance. Thanks to their wise guidance and smart investments, the UAE has transformed into an inspiring success story that proves that knowledge and wise policies are the foundation of progress and prosperity in the modern era.

Today, the UAE stands as a model of progress and development, with a unique architectural renaissance and competitive modern technology on both regional and global levels. Nevertheless, it still preserves its traditional spirit and authentic values, presenting itself today as a model that combines present leadership with historical authenticity. Tradition merges with technology, and the present embraces the past with pride, creating a unique and appealing image that embodies the UAE's journey from simplicity to leadership. The UAE has become an exemplary model in building modern civilization.

At the end of this enchanting journey in the history of the UAE, we realize that the present is the product of the past and a tributary to the future. The modern history of the UAE clearly reflects its pioneering shift towards civilizational renaissance, a success story that inspires the world and forms an unforgettable artistic tableau of progress and innovation.

Today, the UAE is considered a model to be emulated in civilizational renaissance, affirming that determination and hard work can transform the desert into an oasis of creativity and life. With every sunrise, the UAE shines brighter, illuminating the path towards a bright future for its future generations.

Chapter 3

Historical and Cultural Conditions Contributing to the Civilizational Renaissance

The civilizational renaissance is a multifaceted phenomenon influenced by a combination of historical and cultural factors that interact to create an optimal environment for creativity and innovation. The renaissance of any society is linked to its historical transformations and cultural interactions, which is key to deeply understanding the conditions that contributed to the civilizational renaissance. In the case of the United Arab Emirates (UAE), its civilizational renaissance is the result of a unique blend of historical and cultural conditions that have shaped and directed it towards progress and prosperity, which can be outlined as follows:

- **Geographic environment**: The geographical environment is a fundamental factor influencing the growth and development of civilizations. In the case of the UAE, its geographic location in the Middle East makes it a hub for trade and cultural exchange since ancient times. Additionally, the UAE is endowed with diverse natural resources such as oil, gas, and water resources, which have contributed to boosting its economy and developing its infrastructure.

- **Wise leadership**: Wise leadership plays a prominent role in guiding the path of the civilizational renaissance in the UAE. Through ambitious visions and sustainable strategies, Emirati leadership aims to enhance development in various sectors, develop infrastructure, and promote innovation.

- Cultural diversity: The UAE is home to astonishing cultural diversity, where people from various cultures, nationalities, and races live and interact. This diversity enriches social and cultural life, fosters the exchange of experiences and ideas, and promotes development and innovation.

• **Economic development**: Since its independence, the UAE has diversified its economy and developed various sectors, leading to rapid economic growth and financial stability. This economic development has attracted foreign investments, created new job opportunities, improved the standard of living for citizens, and enhanced their capabilities to participate in the process of the civilizational renaissance.

• **Technological advancement**: The UAE has witnessed significant progress in technology, adopting the latest technologies across various sectors, including e-government, artificial intelligence, and digital transformation. This technological advancement enhances efficiency in delivering government services and contributes to achieving the civilizational renaissance.

• **Historical impact and social transformations**: The UAE has experienced important historical transformations, such as the formation of the federation in 1971, adopting an ambitious vision to achieve sustainable development and comprehensive progress. Moreover, the UAE has undergone massive social and economic transformations in recent decades, leading to the emergence of a modern society with remarkable development in various fields.

• **Cultural and religious orientations**: The UAE is characterized by noticeable cultural and religious diversity, with nationals and foreigners from various nationalities and cultures living together. This diversity promotes cultural interaction, enriches social life, enhances understanding and tolerance among different cultures, and fosters innovation and creativity.

The historical and cultural conditions that contributed to the civilizational renaissance in the UAE are among the most important factors that have contributed to progress and development. These conditions have interacted and been managed by wise leadership to transform challenges into opportunities and build a modern society that reflects its commitment to development and progress.

Chapter 4

The Importance of Studying the Civilizational Renaissance in the United Arab Emirates

In the middle of the golden desert, where the blue waves meet the hot sands, the towers of the Emirates rise proudly as a testament to human will and boundless ambition. The UAE, with its rich history and cultural heritage, has been a crossroads of cultures and a cradle of innovation and development, pioneering a distinctive cultural renaissance.

The cultural renaissance is defined as the revival and renewal of ideas, knowledge, sciences, and arts that existed in ancient civilizations, developing and adapting them to current conditions to achieve comprehensive societal progress. The concept of cultural renaissance goes beyond mere economic or technological advancement; it also encompasses the spiritual and moral growth of society. The focus on human values and human rights is an integral part of this renaissance.

Cultural renaissance is not just a specific historical event but a philosophical concept that represents a radical transformation characterized by continuous development and adaptation to social and cultural changes. The features of cultural renaissance can be illustrated through:

•Intellectual renewal: The cultural renaissance is marked by the re-evaluation of prevailing ideas and beliefs, encouraging intellectual dialogue and discussion to reach new and advanced visions.

•Technological advancement: The cultural renaissance shows significant interest in technical innovation and the use of technology to improve quality of life and facilitate daily processes.

•Cultural diversity: The cultural renaissance promotes cultural coexistence and the exchange of knowledge between different peoples and cultures, contributing to the enrichment of human experiences.

•Economic transformation: The cultural renaissance is linked to economic and commercial development, witnessing notable economic growth thanks to improvements in infrastructure and the development of industries.

Therefore, the cultural renaissance is considered a fundamental driver for the progress and development of civilizations, representing a period of innovation and renewal that enhances comprehensive growth and human advancement. The cultural renaissance is not merely a dream or aspiration but an ongoing process that requires continuous efforts and collaboration among all members of society. Through collective work, strong will, and wise leadership, true progress can be achieved, contributing to the elevation of humanity and improving the quality of life for future generations.

The United Arab Emirates is one of the leading countries that has experienced a remarkable cultural renaissance in recent decades. This renaissance has manifested in all aspects of life, whether economic, cultural, educational, or social. Thus, studying this cultural renaissance becomes an imperative necessity to understand the development trajectory the UAE has followed and to aspire to a brighter and more sustainable future. The importance of studying the cultural renaissance in the United Arab Emirates can be illustrated as follows:

Enhancing Cultural and Historical Awareness

Enhancing cultural and historical awareness in the United Arab Emirates is one of the fundamental pillars of building an advanced and distinguished civil society. Studying the cultural renaissance in the UAE is a key element that contributes to deepening this awareness and enhancing the understanding of citizens and residents regarding the country's history and culture.

The cultural renaissance plays a crucial role in building and strengthening national identity among individuals. When people understand the transformations, their country has undergone and the efforts of their ancestors in creating it, they feel a sense of belonging and pride in their history and culture. This positively impacts their engagement with their community and their interaction with various aspects of cultural and social life.

Moreover, studying the cultural renaissance encourages individuals to explore and closely understand the UAE's history, culture, and heritage. It sparks curiosity among people to learn more about the historical roots of the state and its development over time. This fosters a desire to discover more and actively participate in preserving and developing the heritage.

Studying the cultural renaissance in the UAE also contributes to enhancing cultural understanding among citizens and residents of different nationalities and cultures. When individuals have a deep understanding of local customs, traditions, and values, it increases their respect for one another and appreciation of cultural diversity.

Additionally, cultural and historical awareness stimulates innovation and creativity in society. When individuals have a profound understanding of their history and heritage, they can leverage this knowledge to develop new ideas and innovative projects that serve their community and contribute to its development.

The cultural renaissance in the UAE also promotes cultural tourism, attracting tourists worldwide to explore the UAE's history and heritage. This boosts the local economy and contributes to enhancing economic opportunities and sustainable development.

This analysis demonstrates the importance of studying the cultural renaissance in the United Arab Emirates in enhancing cultural and historical awareness, as well as fostering social communication and understanding among different cultures. It is crucial to continue enhancing this awareness by developing diverse and innovative educational and cultural programs, in addition to supporting research and initiatives that contribute to preserving and developing cultural heritage.

Inspiring and motivating new generations

The wise leadership of the UAE, with its inspiring vision, presents a civilized model for transforming the desert into an oasis of creativity and innovation.

The cultural renaissance in the United Arab Emirates is considered a source of inspiration for new generations. It represents a success story that reflects the strength of will and determination to achieve common goals and build a better future for all. From its founding to the present day, the UAE has shown tremendous investment in various economic, cultural, educational, and other fields, making it an example of progress and development.

The cultural renaissance in the Emirates reflects a story of determination and the strong will of the leadership and people to achieve their goals. Through determination and determination to change and develop, the UAE was able to achieve great success and create its distinctive position on the global stage.

The UAE encourages innovation and leadership In all fields, which inspires new generations to take bold and innovative steps in building their future. Innovative thinking and preparation for future challenges is an essential part of the UAE's vision.

The UAE pays great attention to the education and self-development sector, which encourages new generations to continuously learn and acquire modern skills that qualify them to achieve creativity, innovation, and success.

It also calls on young people to assume social responsibility and actively participate in building society and promoting the values of tolerance and peaceful coexistence, which enhances their sense of belonging and responsibility towards their society.

The United Arab Emirates is considered a model of development and progress in the region, and it inspires new generations to realize their dreams and achieve their goals through hard work and innovation. By providing opportunities and providing support to youth, the UAE is building a bright future for future generations.

Strengthening National Identity

Studying the cultural renaissance in the United Arab Emirates plays a significant role in enhancing national identity and fostering a sense of belonging to the country and its progressive civilizational project. This renaissance is not merely about economic or technological achievements; it is also a process of cultural transformation that profoundly impacts national consciousness and attachment to the UAE.

By understanding the immense efforts made to achieve progress and success in various fields, a deeper sense of loyalty and belonging to the UAE as a place to live and work is cultivated.

The study of the cultural renaissance helps build and strengthen national awareness among citizens and residents, as they recognize the extensive efforts and sacrifices made to establish the state and elevate its status on the global stage.

Furthermore, the cultural renaissance encourages the preservation and enhancement of the UAE's cultural identity, thereby fostering a stronger sense of national identity and belonging among community members.

The cultural renaissance also instills a sense of pride and honor in the national achievements of their country across various sectors, reinforcing national identity and attachment to the state.

Additionally, studying the UAE's cultural renaissance stimulates and strengthens the national spirit and solidarity among community members, encouraging active participation in building a promising future for the UAE.

Enhancing national identity in the United Arab Emirates heavily relies on understanding and studying the cultural renaissance and the efforts made to achieve it. It represents a fundamental part of the country's journey towards progress and prosperity and is an integral part of its national identity and sense of belonging.

Attracting Global Investments and Talents

The success achieved by the UAE in various fields reflects a strong appeal for global investments and talents. Consequently, studying the civilizational renaissance can unveil the promising opportunities that the UAE offers to investors and creatives from all over the world. The UAE provides a diverse and open cultural and social environment, which attracts global talents and encourages them to settle and work in the country.

The UAE boasts a proven track record of success in attracting global investments and talents, thanks to its advanced infrastructure, innovative economic policies, and leading business environment. The civilizational renaissance in the UAE is a key factor in this appeal, demonstrating the country's ability to provide a conducive environment for investment and innovation.

The UAE Invests significantly In d"velo'Ing Its infrastructure, including modern international airports, advanced seaports, and sophisticated logistics facilities, creating an ideal environment for investment. It is also considered one of the most attractive countries for investment due to its innovative economic policies, such as economic freedom, flexible regulations, and attractive tax incentives.

Moreover, the wise management of the state in encouraging economic diversification across various sectors—including energy, technology, tourism, and entertainment—offers vast opportunities for international investors. The UAE also promotes innovation, research, and development by investing in innovative sectors and providing a supportive environment for startups and creatives.

Therefore, the United Arab Emirates stands as one of the foremost destinations for global investments and talent. The civilizational renaissance plays a significant role in this appeal by providing an environment conducive to innovation and investment. With ongoing development and progress, the UAE remains an exciting and attractive destination for investors and global talents.

Enhancing Cultural Understanding and Peaceful Coexistence

The civilizational renaissance enhances cultural understanding and peaceful coexistence among the various cultures and nationalities present in the UAE, thereby strengthening community bonds and promoting social harmony .

The United Arab Emirates serves as a model for cultural understanding and peaceful coexistence among different cultures and nationalities, partly due to the civilizational renaissance the country has experienced. This renaissance was not merely an economic and technological transformation but also a cultural and social shift that fostered communication and understanding among the diverse cultures within the UAE.

The driving forces behind the civilizational renaissance in the UAE play a significant role in enhancing cultural understanding and peaceful coexistence. The government has supported educational programs that encourage mutual respect and cultural understanding. Efforts also included comprehensive updates to educational curricula to build a new generation with cultural awareness, tolerance, and the ability to coexist with cultural diversity.

The UAE is considered a global cultural hub that hosts numerous cultural events and festivals, promoting understanding between different cultures. These events encourage cultural exchange and raise awareness about the cultural diversity that characterizes UAE society.

The UAE adopts policies of tolerance that reflect Its commitment to peaceful coexistence among all cultures and nationalities. Cultural understanding and peaceful coexistence are fostered by creating an open society that accepts differences and respects diversity.

The social and economic exchange between different cultures contributes to building bridges of communication and enhancing cultural understanding. The UAE encourages this exchange by establishing free zones and economic areas that attract investors and talents from around the world.

Moreover, the social empowerment model in the UAE encourages the active participation of all groups in economic and social life, thereby enhancing solidarity and cultural understanding among individuals.

Thus, the civilizational renaissance in the UAE is an integral part of enhancing cultural understanding and peaceful coexistence. It highlights the critical role the state plays in promoting tolerance and understanding among its diverse cultures.

Enhancing the Ability to Understand and Overcome Challenges

Delving into the study of the Emirati Renaissance helps in understanding the challenges faced by the country and how it overcame them. The Emirati Renaissance stands as one of the most prominent examples of development and progress in the Middle East and one of the most successful models of growth in the region. The United Arab Emirates transformed from a collection of small emirates into a modern and prosperous state. However, this success was achieved by overcoming significant challenges that the wise government of the UAE tackled with prudent policies and successful strategies. An in-depth study of the challenges faced and how they were overcome provides an opportunity to benefit from the experiences gained in facing future challenges. Some of these challenges include:

• Environmental and Geographical Challenges: Despite being one of the smallest countries in the region, the UAE faces significant geographical and environmental challenges such as scarce water resources and desert terrain. How did the UAE turn these challenges into opportunities for economic development?

• Economic Challenges: Initially, the UAE's economy relied heavily on oil. However, the country faced the challenge of diversifying its income sources to ensure economic sustainability. The transition to a diversified and innovative economy was a real challenge. How did the UAE succeed in promoting innovation and diversifying its income sources to become one of the most economically advanced countries?

• Cultural Challenges: The UAE faced challenges in preserving its cultural identity and traditions. The cultural and demographic diversity posed a significant challenge in building an integrated society. How did the UAE manage to promote peaceful coexistence and utilize this diversity to support economic and social development?

• Social and Human Challenges: Among the significant human challenges were empowering women and achieving gender balance, as well as providing employment and education opportunities for the youth. How did the UAE effectively manage these challenges and involve all segments of society in the development process?

• Political and Security Challenges: The UAE is located in a turbulent region, posing continuous security challenges. How did the UAE, through its prudent security and defense policies, enhance its security and stability to ensure the continuation of its prosperity and civilizational renaissance?

The wise vision and prudent leadership of the UAE's leaders successfully turned challenges into opportunities in the path of development and progress. By focusing on education, and promoting scientific research and innovation, the UAE has built a knowledge-based society that supports sustainable development. Furthermore, strategic partnerships and international cooperation have contributed to enhancing competitiveness and achieving comprehensive development.

The study of the Emirati Renaissance and the analysis of its challenges and the ways they were overcome demonstrate that determination, willpower, and a clear vision are the main factors in achieving sustainable development and success. The UAE has shown exceptional ability to adapt and innovate in facing challenges. Through strategic planning and smart investment, it has achieved remarkable growth and enhanced its position as a global center for business and culture. The UAE continues to strive for a prosperous future that embraces progress while maintaining its deep-rooted heritage.

The civilizational renaissance In the United Arab Emirates serves as an exemplary model of the development and progress that nations can achieve in a short period. It embodies a true success story and forms a source of inspiration for many countries and communities around the world. By studying this renaissance, we can discover how political will and smart investment can radically change the fate of nations, allowing us to benefit from this pioneering and unique experience to build a bright future that ensures prosperity and growth for all.

Chapter 5

The main pillars of the cultural renaissance
In the UAE

In the heart of the desert, where the sands tell the stories of history, the United Arab Emirates emerged as a new chapter in the book of human history, embodied in a remarkable civilizational renaissance. The UAE's journey from simplicity to depth, from desert silence to luxurious modern life, tells a story of human will and determination.

Today, the UAE stands as a symbol of progress and prosperity, one of the shining examples of civilizational renaissance. Guided by wise leadership, it strides confidently towards building a better future and achieving development in various fields. The UAE has shone as a land of opportunities and creativity, its star rising in the world of progress and innovation while preserving its rich heritage and looking towards a bright future. It is a story of renaissance that continues to unfold, promising the world more achievements and wonders. The key pillars of the UAE's civilizational renaissance that have led to its success and development can be outlined as follows:

1. Visionary Leadership

Visionary leadership in the UAE is one of the key pillars that have contributed to the success of the Emirati Renaissance and is a fundamental element in turning vision into tangible reality. It is the secret behind the state's success in achieving sustainable development and progress.

From the outset, the UAE has witnessed continuous civilizational and economic transformation under wise leadership characterized by vision and dedication to progress and development. The Emirati model is a fascinating success story, where wise leadership is manifested in various fields to achieve stability and prosperity for both citizens and residents.

The UAE's leadership has adopted an ambitious vision aimed at transforming the country into a global hub for innovation and leadership in various sectors. This vision has propelled the country towards a bright future. The importance of this vision in the UAE's civilizational renaissance is evident through:

• Strategic Goal Setting: The leadership's vision serves as a strategic reference that outlines the main objectives the state aims to achieve in the long term. By setting these goals, all efforts and resources are directed towards achieving sustainable development and progress in various fields. The wise leadership in the UAE is distinguished by a clear vision and dedication to achieving sustainable strategic goals for development. This vision relies on economic diversification that promotes innovation and balances different sectors.

• Investment Direction: The leadership's vision acts as a driver for directing investments towards priority sectors that contribute to achieving sustainable development goals. Thanks to these directives, the state can efficiently invest its resources to boost the economy and improve the standard of living for its citizens.

• Enhancing International Cooperation: The leadership's vision contributes to enhancing international cooperation and partnerships that benefit the state and society by setting common goals with international partners. The UAE strengthens its position on the international stage and contributes to global sustainable development. The Emirati leadership seeks to build strong international relationships and enhance cooperation in various fields. The UAE enjoys effective diplomacy that fosters international cooperation and helps build strategic global partnerships to achieve global stability and peace. The UAE is also an active partner in global efforts to achieve stability and development.

• Encouraging Innovation and Creativity: Visionary leadership plays a crucial role in stimulating innovation and creativity across various sectors, whether through supporting scientific research or providing a conducive environment for startups and innovators. This contributes to technological advancement and improves the quality of life in the country. The Emirati leadership encourages innovation and entrepreneurship by creating an enabling environment that supports startups and enhances scientific research and technological development. The state invests in talents and provides the necessary opportunities for innovation and creativity. The leadership places great importance on innovation and technological development as drivers of growth, making the UAE home to innovation projects and artificial intelligence initiatives like the "AI City" project in Abu Dhabi.

• Education and Human Development: The UAE's leadership prioritizes investment in education and human development. The state supports high-quality education and advanced educational opportunities for all citizens and residents.

• Achieving Environmental and Social Sustainability: The leadership's vision in the UAE is based on achieving sustainable development in its environmental and social aspects, aiming to balance economic development with the preservation of natural resources and cultural heritage.

Thus, it is clear that the visionary leadership in the UAE is the main driving force behind the state's civilizational renaissance. It is the power that has propelled the country to new levels of development and progress.

2. Education and Development

The education and innovation sector is considered a crucial pillar in the Emirati Renaissance, where the government pays significant attention to its development through supporting investments in education and human development as key milestones of the civilizational uplift. Through the modernization of educational curricula, provision of exceptional educational opportunities, and support for scientific research, the UAE has successfully built an innovative and distinguished generation that contributes to progress and prosperity.

In modern UAE, educational and developmental institutions have played a vital role in laying the foundations of civilization and enhancing the country's economic and social renaissance. These institutions are a backbone in realizing the UAE's vision for a prosperous and sustainable future.

Investments in education and human development are fundamental to any country's civilizational renaissance. Education is the sole path to building an educated, innovative, and advanced society, significantly contributing to societal progress and prosperity. In this context, the United Arab Emirates stands out as a shining example due to its substantial investments in education and development, which have helped cultivate an innovative and distinguished generation, fostering innovation and sustainable development.

The UAE began its journey towards civilizational transformation by updating and developing educational curricula to align with the requirements of the modern age. Educational materials that encourage critical thinking, innovation, and the development of communication and teamwork skills were included, aiming to prepare students to efficiently and confidently face future challenges.

The importance of exceptional education in the Emirates is also reflected in providing diverse and outstanding educational opportunities for all. The Emirati government has provided exceptional educational opportunities for the youth by establishing world-class universities, colleges, and advanced research centers. An inspiring and motivating educational environment has been provided, encouraging continuous learning and innovation.

Attention is also given to students with special needs by providing an inclusive and supportive educational environment. The UAE strives to empower every individual to realize their full potential and contribute to achieving sustainable development.

Scientific research has been encouraged, and investments have been directed towards research and development areas, contributing to the development of innovative solutions for modern challenges.

In addition, the UAE places significant emphasis on supporting scientific research, encouraging innovation, and fostering entrepreneurship. By providing the necessary platforms and resources, researchers and innovators are empowered to develop innovative solutions for current and future challenges, driving the country's civilizational progress and enhancing its global competitiveness in various fields.

Education and development form a fundamental pillar of the civilizational renaissance in the Emirates, where substantial investments in knowledge and human resources represent the true wealth of the state and the key to achieving sustainable development and comprehensive prosperity.

3. Economic Diversification

Economic diversification is considered one of the most important foundations of the civilizational renaissance in the UAE. Thanks to the economic diversification strategy, the UAE's economy has been transformed from reliance on oil to a multi-sector economy, attracting investments and advancing sustainable development.

The United Arab Emirates represents a leading model in the world of economic diversification, having managed to transform its economy from total dependence on oil and gas to a diversified multi-sector economy. With the main economic diversification strategy, economic resilience has been enhanced, and opportunities for sustainable development and comprehensive prosperity in society have been maximized.

Historically, the UAE relied heavily on oil and gas exports to generate income and fund development projects. With the growing awareness of the importance of economic diversification and the need to reduce total dependence on oil, the UAE began taking decisive steps towards diversifying its economic base. This diversification aims to mitigate the impact of oil price fluctuations, provide diverse job opportunities, and increase and diversify income sources, thereby strengthening the national economy.

One of the most prominent areas that have seen tremendous development is the tourism and hospitality sector, thanks to significant investments in developing tourist resorts and attractions. The UAE has attracted millions of tourists annually from all over the world, contributing to diversifying income sources and enhancing economic balance.

In addition to tourism, the UAE has seen significant growth in other sectors such as technology, education, financial services, trade, and light industries. Through the establishment of free zones and special economic zones, entrepreneurship has been encouraged, and global companies have been attracted to reside and invest in the UAE.

The UAE is also considered an ideal environment for innovation and entrepreneurship, where it encourages and supports startups and innovators in various sectors. Thanks to this encouragement, the UAE is experiencing rapid growth in the innovation sector and the development of modern technologies, contributing to progress and prosperity.

Furthermore, the UAE is working to attract foreign investments by providing a favorable investment environment and advanced facilities supportive of investment. In addition, the UAE government invests heavily in infrastructure and service development, making the UAE an attractive place for local and international investments.

Today, the UAE embodies an inspiring model of successful economic diversification, leading to enhanced economic resilience and sustainable development. With continued commitment to innovation and improving the business environment, the UAE can continue to achieve success on its path towards economic prosperity.

Economic diversification is considered a fundamental pillar of the civilizational renaissance in the UAE, which has contributed to achieving economic, social, and cultural stability for the country.

4. Technology and Innovation

The role of technology and innovation in driving economic growth and achieving global leadership cannot be overlooked. This sector holds a prominent place in propelling progress and economic development in the United Arab Emirates, where it is considered one of the key sectors and the fundamental pillar for achieving global leadership and enhancing sustainable development. Through substantial investments in the fields of technology and innovation, the UAE has succeeded in building a knowledge-based economy reliant on new ideas and innovations, contributing to enhanced international competitiveness and sustainable economic growth.

The UAE boasts an advanced technological infrastructure, providing the necessary digital infrastructure to support technology and innovation. Through the development of high-speed communication networks and extensive wireless coverage, companies and individuals are enabled to access technology and information quickly and reliably.

The UAE's efforts in developing technological infrastructure have included numerous significant projects such as Masdar City, artificial intelligence initiatives, and digital transformation in government and the private sector. The UAE strives to provide a conducive environment for tech companies and encourage innovation, optimizing the use of technology in all aspects of life.

The UAE also pays great attention to supporting innovation and entrepreneurship, ensuring an encouraging and supportive environment for startups and innovators. By establishing free zones for technology and advanced research centers, the necessary platforms are provided for developing and marketing innovations and transforming them into widely applicable products and services.

Furthermore, the UAE government supports innovative projects and startups by providing funding, space, and resources necessary for growth and development. It encourages knowledge exchange and collaboration between the public and private sectors to foster innovation and develop technological solutions capable of addressing economic and social challenges.

The UAE also relies on strategic partnerships with global companies in the fields of technology and innovation, working to attract global talent and expertise for knowledge exchange and innovation enhancement.

By directing investments towards technology-based economic sectors such as artificial intelligence, big data analytics, and nanotechnologies, the UAE aims to boost its competitive capabilities and achieve sustainable development in the era of the knowledge economy.

Technology and innovation constitute two fundamental pillars of leadership and progress in the UAE, with these sectors being a primary driver for achieving comprehensive prosperity and building a prosperous future.

5. Advanced Infrastructure

A civilization's renaissance cannot be complete without advanced infrastructure that supports economic growth and meets societal needs. Through massive investments in airports, ports, roads, telecommunications, and energy, the UAE has built an advanced infrastructure befitting its cultural stature.

Advanced infrastructure is one of the most critical factors for any nation's success and prosperity, playing a decisive role in supporting economic growth and achieving sustainable development. In this context, the United Arab Emirates stands out as a model for building advanced infrastructure that meets societal needs and enhances its cultural position on the international stage.

Through substantial investments in various infrastructure sectors, the UAE has turned its economic vision into a tangible reality that reflects future aspirations, attracts investments, and promotes comprehensive development. This advanced infrastructure encompasses a wide range of projects and facilities that ensure the provision of essential services and enhance sustainability in the UAE.

One of the most important elements of advanced infrastructure in the UAE is the airport sector, with the country hosting leading international airports such as Dubai International Airport and Abu Dhabi International Airport. These airports serve as main gateways for air connectivity with the world, boosting tourism, and international trade, and supporting economic growth.

Additionally, the UAE boasts an advanced maritime infrastructure with world-class ports like Jebel Ali Port in Dubai and Khor Fakkan Port in Sharjah. These ports reinforce the country's role as a maritime trade hub and contribute to global economic integration.

The role of advanced infrastructure extends beyond transportation to include roads and land transport networks. The UAE has a modern and developed road network connecting various cities and industrial areas, facilitating the movement of goods and people and enhancing social and economic connectivity.

With technological advancements, the UAE enjoys a developed telecommunications infrastructure that includes high-speed internet networks and advanced wireless coverage. This infrastructure supports innovation and the technology sector.

Lastly, energy is a fundamental aspect of advanced infrastructure, and the UAE has significant capabilities in producing clean energy such as solar and nuclear power. This contributes to enhancing environmental sustainability and providing sustainable energy sources for the future.

Advanced infrastructure is considered a pillar of prosperity in the UAE's cultural renaissance, reflecting the country's commitment to achieving sustainable development and economic and social progress.

6. Sustainable Development and Environmental Protection

In an era where the environment is a fundamental pillar of sustainable development, the United Arab Emirates stands as a prominent example of commitment to environmental protection and achieving development in a manner that respects nature and preserves its resources. The UAE has provided a model for the world in balancing economic growth with environmental protection. The country places significant emphasis on sustainable development and environmental protection, implementing policies and programs to conserve natural resources and minimize the negative environmental impacts of its economic activities.

The UAE relies on multiple strategies to achieve sustainable development, integrating environmental protection into its economic and social goals. Based on this principle, the UAE invests in information technology and renewable energy projects and encourages innovation in environmental and energy sectors.

Through technology and innovation, the UAE develops and adopts modern technologies to protect the environment and reduce the negative impacts of its economic activities. The government strives to enhance energy efficiency and promote the use of renewable energy sources, such as solar, wind, and safe nuclear energy. The government also encourages innovation in clean energy and the development of environmental technologies to preserve the environment and achieve sustainable development.

Education and awareness about environmental issues are top priorities for the UAE. The country organizes awareness campaigns and educational programs targeting youth and civil society to enhance awareness of the importance of the environment and the necessity of preserving it for future generations.

The UAE adopts advanced strategies in sustainable structural development by promoting smart and sustainable buildings, developing smart and integrated cities, and improving the quality of life for its citizens. Projects such as Masdar City, Global Village, and green tourism development projects exemplify the UAE's commitment to sustainable structural development.

The UAE also pays special attention to protecting natural resources, both terrestrial and aquatic, by launching initiatives to preserve biodiversity, provide green spaces, and improve water and air quality.

Additionally, the UAE makes continuous efforts to combat climate change and reduce harmful emissions.

The UAE seeks to enhance international cooperation in environmental protection, participating in global initiatives and emphasizing the importance of international collaboration to address global environmental challenges.

The UAE's efforts in environmental protection and sustainable development demonstrate a serious and practical commitment to achieving sustainable development goals through investment in technology, awareness, and international cooperation. The UAE serves as a successful model in the field of sustainability, inspiring the world.

7. Security and Political Stability

The United Arab Emirates is one of the most stable and secure countries in the Arabian Gulf. Security and political stability are fundamental pillars in building the UAE's civilizational renaissance, creating a conducive environment for sustainable development, investment, and international cooperation.

The UAE serves as a model of leadership and excellence on both regional and international levels in the areas of security and stability. Through its ambitious vision and wise leadership, the UAE has built a strong, economically prosperous, and politically stable state over the past five decades in a record period. Among the foundations of this success, the role of security and stability is a decisive factor in achieving prosperity and progress. Over the many years, the UAE has achieved numerous significant accomplishments in the field of security and political stability, making it a global model to be emulated.

The importance of security and political stability is highlighted as one of the main factors affecting the economic and social development of any country. In the case of the UAE, strong political stability enhances confidence among local and international investors, contributing to economic growth and providing job opportunities for citizens.

The UAE's achievements in security and stability have been reflected in a variety of areas, leading to significant progress. The size of the national economy has risen markedly from 15 billion dollars in 1975 to nearly 430 billion dollars at present. Social stability and peaceful coexistence among different cultures, religions, and ethnicities have also been achieved in the UAE.

Despite these significant achievements, the UAE faces multiple challenges, including terrorist threats, regional challenges, and global geopolitical shifts. To address these challenges, the state must adopt comprehensive and integrated strategies to ensure the continuation of security and stability.

To achieve security and stability, the UAE is developing internal policies that enhance the partnership between the government and civil society and achieve a balance between rights and duties.

Therefore, the UAE adopts a firm policy in the field of security and stability, where the government attaches great importance to enhancing laws and regulations that preserve order and ensure social peace. It also promotes justice and strictly applies the law to ensure the safety and security of all its citizens and residents.

On the international stage, the UAE underscores the importance of international cooperation in combating terrorism and enhancing regional and global security. The UAE believes in the significance of international cooperation in security and stability and strives to strengthen regional and international partnerships to address common security challenges. Consequently, the UAE actively participates in international efforts to combat terrorism and enhance regional and global security.

The UAE's advanced foreign policy focuses on fostering relationships and achieving international cooperation, aiming to manage conflicts constructively and build strong partnerships with friendly and allied nations.

The United Arab Emirates remains a symbol of security and stability in the Gulf region and globally. Through its commitment to enhancing security and stability, the UAE continues to lead in achieving progress and prosperity in a changing world, turning challenges into opportunities for development and advancement.

8. Social Balance and Human Development

In a world facing increasing social challenges, the United Arab Emirates stands out as a leading model for social balance and human development. The UAE is earnestly committed to promoting balance and equity among all segments of society by providing opportunities, enhancing human rights, and developing civil society.

The UAE's strategy for social balance is based on the principles of sustainable development and social justice. This balance is achieved through investments in education, job creation, human rights enhancement, and civil society development.

The UAE ensures equal opportunities for all members of society through educational and training policies and programs that enhance skills and provide employment opportunities for youth and women. The government adopts policies that encourage equal opportunities and promote economic development for all age and social groups.

Human rights are an integral part of the UAE's vision for social development. The country works on developing legislation and policies that ensure the protection of human rights and promote the principles of justice and equality.

The UAE also encourages the development of civil society and enhances its role by promoting democracy and community participation. The government supports community initiatives and encourages active citizen participation in decision-making.

The UAE's efforts to promote social balance and achieve human development reflect a serious commitment to the principles of justice and equality. By balancing opportunities, ensuring human rights, and developing civil society, the UAE is moving towards a more prosperous and progressive society.

Chapter 6

The Urban Renaissance in the United Arab Emirates

The United Arab Emirates is experiencing a remarkable urban renaissance that is an integral part of a wise vision aimed at achieving sustainable development and prosperity in various fields. This renaissance reflects the comprehensive transformation and urban growth that Emirati cities have witnessed over the decades, transitioning from orchards and deserts to modern and innovative urban centers.

In the context of the UAE, the urban renaissance signifies the comprehensive transformation and development of cities and urban infrastructure, which includes the expansion of cities and the construction of modern facilities such as residential, commercial, and government buildings, as well as the establishment of essential infrastructure like roads, bridges, transportation networks, and services.

The architectural renaissance in the development of cities and communities is one of the most important factors contributing to urban development and enhancing the quality of life for citizens and residents. It is associated with numerous benefits and advantages, including:

•Improvement of Infrastructure: The architectural renaissance involves providing modern and advanced infrastructure, which contributes to improving community services such as healthcare, education, and transportation.

•Increase in Job Opportunities: Urban development creates new job opportunities in the construction, real estate, and infrastructure-related service sectors.

•Enhancement of the Local Economy: Urban growth stimulates economic activity, boosts investments, supports the local economy, and contributes to comprehensive development.

•Promotion of Tourism Appeal: Developed and modern cities attract tourists and enhance the positive image of the country on an international level.

•Improvement in Welfare and Quality of Life: Urban development improves the quality of life for residents by providing a comfortable and integrated urban environment.

The architectural renaissance in the UAE plays a vital role in developing communities and enhancing economic and social stability, reflecting the government's commitment to achieving an innovative and sustainable future vision.

The Key Factors of the Urban Renaissance in the UAE

The Wise Vision of the Emirati Leadership

The wise vision of the Emirati leadership is one of the most significant driving factors of this urban renaissance, leading to exceptional achievements in urban development and improving the quality of life for citizens and residents. The United Arab Emirates has witnessed a notable urban renaissance that reflects the comprehensive transformation experienced by Emirati cities and regions, represented by a tremendous urban and economic shift over the years.

The wise vision of the UAE's leadership is the fundamental element behind the prominent success of the urban and civilizational renaissance. This vision enhances the comprehensive transformation that Emirati cities and regions have undergone over the years. It aims to achieve progress and sustainable development, turning the vision into a tangible reality that enhances the stability and well-being of citizens and residents.

From the outset, the UAE has continuously experienced a civilizational and economic transformation, thanks to wise leadership characterized by vision and dedication to progress. The UAE is an admirable model of wise leadership, inspiring stability and well-being for both citizens and residents. The aspects of this wise vision can be illustrated through the policies adopted by the government, as follows:

• Transitioning towards sustainable development: The wise vision of the Emirati leadership is a primary motivator for the transition towards sustainable development. The Emirati leadership has set ambitious strategies and plans to achieve comprehensive development across all sectors, including infrastructure. Through this vision, urban development priorities have been identified, and investments have been effectively directed towards infrastructure development projects.

• Investing in urban infrastructure: The wise vision is a key factor in directing investments towards the development of urban infrastructure in the Emirates. Emirati cities have seen the construction of massive projects, including luxurious residential buildings, modern commercial complexes, advanced public transport facilities, and high-level health and educational facilities. All these projects result from the strategic vision set by the Emirati leadership to achieve comprehensive development and community well-being.

• Supporting innovation and sustainability: The wise vision promotes support for innovation and sustainability in infrastructure development, encouraging technological and sustainable environmental initiatives. The UAE utilizes advanced technology such as artificial intelligence and the Internet to improve infrastructure and provide better services to citizens and residents.

Economic Development and Population Growth

The United Arab Emirates is among the nations that have experienced a significant economic transformation over the past decades, and this economic development has played a crucial role in supporting population growth and achieving comprehensive progress in the urban renaissance. The exciting interaction between economic development and population growth can be seen as a driving factor for the urban renaissance in the UAE.

As one of the leading oil-producing countries in the world, the discovery of oil and gas brought about a profound transformation in the national economy. However, the government diversified the economy through investments in tourism, trade, technology, and innovation. This economic diversification led to strong and sustainable economic growth, enhancing the state's financial capabilities to fund large urban projects.

With economic development, the UAE has seen tremendous population growth due to the attraction of expatriate labor and an increase in local birth rates. This rapid and sustained population growth posed challenges to the existing infrastructure, prompting the government to invest significantly in developing urban infrastructure and public services to keep pace with the continuous population growth. The impact of population growth and economic development on the urban and civilizational renaissance can be demonstrated through the following points:

• Development of modern cities: Economic development and population growth have led to the development of modern cities in the UAE, such as Dubai and Abu Dhabi. These cities have seen the construction of high-quality and advanced residential and commercial buildings that meet the needs of residents and investors.

• Improvement of urban infrastructure: The government has comprehensively developed urban infrastructure, such as building roads, bridges, public transportation networks, and health and educational facilities, to meet the growing needs of the population.

• Enhancement of tourism and economic appeal: Economic development and population growth have enhanced the tourism and economic appeal of the UAE, leading to increased foreign investment and economic prosperity.

Economic development and population growth are considered key factors that have contributed to the urban renaissance in the UAE, leading to the comprehensive and sustainable development of cities and communities over the years.

Government Investments in Infrastructure

Government investments in infrastructure are a fundamental element and a major driver of the notable urban renaissance in the United Arab Emirates. These serious and continuous investments are an essential part of the strategic vision of the Emirati leadership to achieve development and sustainable progress in various vital areas, including infrastructure. The importance of government investments in infrastructure is evident through:

• Improving quality and efficiency: Government investments contribute to improving the quality and efficiency of infrastructure, enhancing services provided to citizens and residents, and improving the standard of living.

• Boosting the Economy: Advanced infrastructure attracts both foreign and domestic investments, stimulating economic growth and enhancing economic competitiveness.

• Supporting vital sectors: Investments contribute to the development of vital sectors such as transportation, energy, and communications, enhancing economic and social integration.

• Stimulating sustainable development: Government investments promote sustainability by adopting modern and advanced technologies that balance development and environmental conservation.

Government investments in infrastructure in the UAE vary in several areas:

• Roads and transportation: The UAE possesses an advanced network of roads, airports, and ports, reflecting the government's commitment to improving and developing transportation infrastructure.

• Energy: The Emirati government invests in renewable energy generation projects and the development of distribution networks to meet the increasing energy demand.

• Communications: The government is developing communication networks and providing high-speed internet services to support innovation and technological advancement.

The impact of government investments on the urban renaissance is evident in:

• Achieving social and economic balance: Investments contribute to achieving a balance between urban and rural areas, enhancing employment opportunities and economic growth.

• Attracting foreign investments: Advanced infrastructure enhances the country's attractiveness for foreign investments, contributing to comprehensive development.

The Development of Cities and Urban Areas in the UAE

Modern Architecture and Cultural Heritage

Modern architecture and cultural heritage in the United Arab Emirates represent an important element of the human renaissance in the country, reflecting an ideal balance between civilizational development and the retention of the community's cultural and historical identity. The focus on modern architectural construction that respects cultural heritage reflects a futuristic vision that integrates modernity with tradition.

In recent decades, the UAE has embarked on massive urban projects that reflect technological advancement and innovation in the field of architectural engineering. The Emirates is known for its towering skyscrapers and innovative buildings that are symbols of development and economic prosperity. Nevertheless, preserving cultural and architectural heritage remains a priority for the Emirati government.

An example of this is the Sharjah Urban Design project, which combines traditional and modern elements in design, focusing on the use of local materials and traditional construction techniques. Additionally, initiatives to rehabilitate historical and heritage sites such as the Fujairah Historic Village and Al Ain Heritage Village represent an investment in the past to enhance cultural and heritage awareness among the public.

Efforts in the field of modern architecture and cultural heritage are part of a comprehensive strategy to enhance the human renaissance in the Emirates, contributing to enriching the urban environment and enhancing national belonging and identity. Moreover, modern architecture plays a pivotal role in enhancing the image of the Emirates as a global tourist and investment destination that harmoniously and attractively blends history with modernity.

The Evolution of Abu Dhabi: A Cultural and Economic Capital

The development of Abu Dhabi as a cultural and economic capital in the UAE stands as a remarkable example of urban transformation and rapid development witnessed by the city over the past decades. Today, Abu Dhabi boasts a dynamic and vibrant community that blends ancient culture with modern technological advancements.

The history of urban development in Abu Dhabi dates back to the independence of the United Arab Emirates in 1971. At that time, the city relied primarily on fishing and agriculture, but the government swiftly began diversifying its economy thanks to its rich oil and gas resources.

One of the most significant projects in Abu Dhabi is the "Saadiyat Island" development, which hosts a collection of important cultural institutions such as the "Louvre Abu Dhabi" and the "Islamic Art Museum." These projects have played a significant role in enhancing the city's status as a global cultural destination.

Furthermore, Abu Dhabi has witnessed tremendous growth in the tourism and entertainment sectors, with the establishment of tourist attractions such as "Ferrari World" and "Zayed Sports City." These projects aim to attract tourists and investors while promoting economic diversity.

Abu Dhabi has also invested heavily in technology and innovation, applying advanced techniques in fields such as artificial intelligence and renewable energy. These initiatives reflect the city's commitment to sustainability and technological progress.

The evolution of Abu Dhabi serves as an ideal model for sustainable and balanced urban transformation, as the government seeks to achieve comprehensive development and provide an excellent quality of life for its citizens and residents. Today, Abu Dhabi stands as one of the most important cultural and economic hubs in the region, continuing to pursue future aspirations for growth and prosperity.

Dubai: A Model of Transformation from Desert to Global City

The evolution of cities and urban areas in the UAE, particularly in Dubai, represents a prominent model of urban transformation that blends traditional allure with modern technologies, transforming the Emirates' desert into a global destination characterized by innovation and economic vibrancy. Dubai is distinguished by its rapid and sustainable development, reflecting the UAE's ability to adapt and evolve in the face of environmental and economic challenges.

Initially, Dubai was a barren desert located on the Arabian Gulf coast. The significant transformation began in the 1970s and 1980s when the UAE took steps towards economic diversification, focusing on tourism, trade, and services. Over the years, prudent government investment policies led to rapid growth in infrastructure and pioneering real estate projects.

One of Dubai's most iconic developments is the Burj Khalifa project, the tallest building in the world, symbolizing ambition and architectural innovation. Additionally, Dubai has witnessed tremendous growth in tourism and hospitality, offering a diverse array of luxury resorts and cultural landmarks.

Dubai's economic success and ongoing development are attributed to the wise vision of leadership and innovative developmental strategies, including support for innovation and entrepreneurship and providing a conducive investment environment. Today, Dubai represents a global hub for business, trade, and culture, with continued investment in smart and sustainable projects.

The story of Dubai's transformation from desert to global prominence is a widely inspiring lesson in urban planning and sustainable development. This story reflects the ability to achieve change and fulfill ambitions, inspiring many cities and communities around the world to explore similar paths of development.

The Emirate of Sharjah

The Emirate of Sharjah in the United Arab Emirates stands out as a leading model for urban development and sustainable growth in the region. Sharjah began its journey towards urban transformation and development decades ago, achieving significant success in developing infrastructure, enhancing culture and heritage, and supporting a diverse economy.

Sharjah reflects a strategic vision for sustainable urban development, witnessing the creation of modern projects that include housing, roads, and public facilities. This development aims to provide a comfortable and sustainable environment for both residents and visitors.

Currently, the emirate is experiencing significant urban growth that reflects its ongoing commitment to development and innovation in infrastructure and architecture. Sharjah, one of the emirates of the United Arab Emirates, is renowned for its rich cultural legacy and dedication to supporting the arts and culture. The Emirate of Sharjah adopts an ambitious strategic vision focused on enhancing urban life and boosting the emirate's tourism and economic appeal.

Sharjah has seen significant infrastructure development, including the construction of modern and advanced facilities such as residential, commercial, and entertainment complexes. This includes the creation of modern shopping centers, museums, and art galleries that reflect the emirate's cultural identity.

The Emirate of Sharjah is implementing numerous key strategic government projects, such as road improvement and transportation projects, and the construction of schools, hospitals, and health facilities.

Sharjah is a leader in sustainable development, housing many innovative and sustainable environmental projects. For example, the "Sharjah Sustainable City Project" was launched, aiming to enhance sustainability in urban planning and provide a sustainable and healthy environment for the population.

Sharjah is considered the cultural capital of the Arab world, hosting numerous cultural, artistic, and literary festivals. The emirate also boasts many museums and exhibitions that highlight Arab and Islamic heritage. Sharjah also pays special attention to preserving the tangible and intangible heritage of the region.

Sharjah places great emphasis on enhancing cultural and artistic life. The emirate regularly organizes various cultural and artistic events, such as book festivals, art exhibitions, and musical performances, enhancing Sharjah's international status as a prominent cultural destination in the region.

These comprehensive efforts reflect the Emirate of Sharjah's commitment to sustainable development and achieving an ambitious vision for the future, harmoniously blending tradition and modernity. Such a strategic approach is fundamental to making Sharjah one of the most attractive destinations for living and working.

The Emirate of Ajman

The urban renaissance in Ajman represents an exceptional journey of urban development in a small yet ambitious emirate in the United Arab Emirates. Despite its small geographical size, Ajman has witnessed a notable urban renaissance reflecting comprehensive development in infrastructure and urban planning.

In recent years, the Emirate of Ajman has experienced significant growth and development in various urban aspects. Among the factors contributing to this development is the innovative and wise vision of the government leadership, which strives to improve the quality of life for the emirate's residents and enhance infrastructure to support sustainable growth.

Today, the emirate stands as an inspiring model for urban renaissance in the region, with some of the prominent aspects of this renaissance being:

• Advanced urban planning, where the Emirate of Ajman adopts a clear strategic vision for urban planning, aiming to develop cities sustainably and orderly. The residential and commercial areas are witnessing notable development, with a focus on establishing vital facilities such as commercial, recreational, and cultural zones.

• Developed infrastructure, where Ajman's infrastructure sector is experiencing significant improvements, including road networks and public facilities like schools, hospitals, and recreational areas.

Investments in these areas are one of the reasons for the tangible progress in the urban renaissance.

• Major and innovative projects, as Ajman has seen the implementation of numerous major and innovative projects that enhance the architectural and economic identity of the emirate. Among these projects is the "City of Flowers" project, which aims to create a sustainable community surrounded by nature.

• The role of innovation and technology, technology and innovation are essential parts of Ajman's urban renaissance, as the emirate adopts smart and innovative solutions in various fields such as energy and smart infrastructure.

This urban development in Ajman serves as a successful model for urban transformation in the region, combining wise leadership vision with sustainability, technology, and comprehensive planning to achieve societal and economic progress. This urban renaissance serves as a source of inspiration for other regions striving for sustainable growth and integrated urban development.

The Emirate of Ras Al Khaimah

The Emirate of Ras Al Khaimah is currently witnessing a significant urban renaissance that reflects its ongoing commitment to development and improvement in the areas of infrastructure and urbanization. Ras Al Khaimah is one of the emirates known for its stunning natural beauty and strategic location on the Arabian Gulf coast.

The emirate has undergone a remarkable transformation in recent years, with the launch of several large-scale urban projects. These projects include the construction of modern residential complexes and the development of infrastructure to enhance the quality of life and meet the needs of residents.

Additionally, Ras Al Khaimah is considered a diverse and attractive tourist destination. It focuses on developing the tourism and entertainment sectors, with nature and the local environment being among the prominent sustainable resources. RAK attracts tourists from around the world thanks to its attractive areas such as Jebel Jais and Al Hamra Island. Tourists also enjoy opportunities to experience the stunning sandy beaches and various water activities. Resorts and tourist areas have been developed to increase the emirate's appeal to incoming tourists.

The Emirate of Ras Al Khaimah is committed to developing infrastructure to improve the quality of services provided to citizens and residents. These efforts include the development of road and transportation networks, the construction of modern hospitals and schools, and the provision of sports and recreational facilities.

In addition to urban development, Ras Al Khaimah pays attention to preserving its cultural and historical heritage, organizing cultural and artistic events to raise awareness of local heritage, and promoting traditional arts.

The government of Ras Al Khaimah is implementing numerous strategic government projects aimed at supporting economic and social development. These projects include investments in industry, technology, and tourism.

The urban renaissance in Ras Al Khaimah reflects the emirate's commitment to sustainable development and improving the quality of life for its inhabitants. These efforts are based on an ambitious strategic vision aimed at making Ras Al Khaimah an ideal place to live and invest.

Sustainable Development and Environment

Environmental Initiatives in Urban Planning

The United Arab Emirates adopts environmental initiatives in urban planning as a fundamental part of its vision for sustainable and environmental development. The UAE strives to achieve a balance between urban development and the preservation of the natural environment, providing a healthy and sustainable living environment for its citizens and residents.

The UAE invests in the development and use of advanced environmental technology in urban planning. This is exemplified by the implementation of renewable energy systems such as solar and wind power in urban projects, and the use of green building technologies that reduce carbon emissions and improve energy consumption efficiency.

Moreover, the UAE lays out sustainable plans for city development, focusing on providing green spaces and designing buildings in ways that enhance their sustainability. This includes the use of eco-friendly building materials and the provision of pedestrian walkways and public transportation.

Water resources are among the most significant environmental challenges in the region, so the UAE ensures the application of water conservation strategies and seawater desalination to meet the future needs of cities.

The UAE is concerned with increasing environmental awareness in society, organizing awareness campaigns and educational programs aimed at encouraging citizens and residents to adopt sustainable and environmentally friendly lifestyles.

Furthermore, the UAE implements pioneering environmental projects such as the "Masdar City Environmental Reserve," which embodies efforts to preserve biodiversity and the environment.

These initiatives are part of the UAE's firm commitment to sustainable development and environmental protection, reflecting the pioneering spirit in applying the concepts of comprehensive and sustainable development in the planning and development of cities.

Resource and Energy Sustainability in Emirati Cities

The sustainability of resources and energy in Emirati cities is a fundamental part of the United Arab Emirates' efforts towards sustainable and environmental development. The UAE is distinguished by its adoption of advanced strategies for resource management and energy efficiency, aiming to enhance the quality of life and preserve the environment.

The UAE is working towards diversifying energy sources beyond a total reliance on fossil fuels. It possesses significant potential in the field of renewable energy, especially solar and wind power, and invests heavily in developing renewable energy projects.

The UAE adopts modern technologies to increase energy efficiency in cities, through the implementation of smart lighting systems and energy control and enhancing the use of environmental technology in buildings and facilities.

Water management is a vital issue in the region, and the UAE pays great attention to improving water use efficiency and applying desalination and recycling technologies to conserve water resources.

The UAE also adopts sustainable urban designs, which include the use of green spaces, providing advanced public transportation, and enhancing sustainability in the structure of cities and community planning.

The UAE invests in innovation and scientific research to develop new technologies in the field of resource and energy sustainability and encourages international cooperation to exchange knowledge and successful experiences.

Resource and energy sustainability is an essential part of the UAE's Vision 2030 for sustainable development, and the ongoing efforts in this field represent a vital investment to achieve better sustainable and environmental development in Emirati cities.

Infrastructure and Modern Facilities

Road Networks and Urban Transportation

Road networks and urban transportation are considered among the most crucial elements of the advanced infrastructure in the UAE, contributing to enhanced mobility and ease of movement within and between cities. The UAE is committed to developing and improving this infrastructure to enhance the quality of life, sustainability, and the economy.

The UAE boasts a modern and advanced road network, including highways and main roads that connect major cities and regions. The country invests in expanding and upgrading this network to keep pace with the growing population and economic development.

Urban transportation is essential for improving the mobility of citizens and residents in cities. The UAE employs modern technologies in developing public transportation projects such as metro systems and smart buses, aiming to provide comfortable and efficient transport services.

Additionally, the UAE utilizes technology in transportation management, such as smartphone applications for booking and tracking transit, and intelligent traffic signal systems to improve traffic flow and reduce congestion.

The UAE also undertakes major projects in transportation, such as airport developments, the creation of integrated transportation hubs, and modern seaports, to strengthen its role as a global transportation and trade center.

Moreover, the country is achieving a shift towards smart transportation by adopting intelligent and sustainable transportation systems that leverage modern technologies to increase transportation efficiency and reduce negative environmental impacts.

These efforts to improve road networks and urban transportation are a fundamental part of the UAE's strategy to promote sustainable development and achieve a balance between economic growth and environmental preservation.

Developments in the Healthcare Sector

The UAE has witnessed a significant transformation in the healthcare sector over the past few years, with substantial investments in infrastructure development and the improvement of healthcare facilities. This transformation encompasses several key aspects:

In the realm of modern healthcare facilities, we find:

•Advanced hospitals and medical centers, such as the Cleveland Clinic Abu Dhabi and Dubai's Medical Center Hospital. These facilities are renowned for providing high-quality healthcare services and specialized care across various medical disciplines.

•Modern healthcare technologies, with the UAE adopting advanced technologies such as artificial intelligence and personalized medicine to enhance diagnostic accuracy and treatment efficacy.

•Comprehensive community healthcare, as the UAE has expanded health coverage and improved access to healthcare services for both citizens and residents.

•Innovation and medical research, through supporting innovation in healthcare, investing in medical research, and establishing leading centers for medical innovation.

In the area of digital transformation in healthcare, we observe:

•A shift towards digital health, with the UAE offering advanced digital health services, including smart health applications and online medical consultations.

•The electronic health record (EHR), with the implementation of an EHR system that facilitates the exchange of medical information among healthcare providers.

In terms of investment in medical education and training, we find:

•Development of qualified healthcare professionals, with the UAE offering exceptional educational programs to train both local and international healthcare professionals.

•Collaboration with global universities, as the UAE has partnered with international universities to provide advanced training and educational programs in medicine and health sciences.

The remarkable developments in the UAE's healthcare sector reflect the country's commitment to advancing and evolving healthcare services, inspired by its ambitious vision to ensure community well-being and health. These efforts embody a comprehensive strategic vision to achieve high-quality healthcare standards and integrate modern technological advancements in this field.

Developments in the Educational Sector

The developments in the educational sector in the UAE represent a model of comprehensive transformation and continuous progress in enhancing educational infrastructure and providing modern facilities that meet the growing needs of the community. The UAE is a leader in education in the Middle East, striving to develop an exceptional educational environment based on the latest technologies and global standards.

Regarding the transformations and developments in the educational sector, we observe:

•Advanced infrastructure: The UAE has built modern, technologically equipped schools that provide an ideal learning environment. These schools include multi-purpose facilities, such as advanced science laboratories and digital libraries.

•Integration of technology in education: The UAE aims to incorporate technology into education by providing smart devices to students and developing innovative e-learning platforms to enhance the learning process.

•Offering diverse and advanced educational programs: Various educational programs are provided, including vocational education, university education, and professional training, to meet the changing needs of the labor market.

•Collaboration with global universities: The UAE has established partnerships with prestigious international universities to offer joint study programs and exchange knowledge and expertise in multiple fields.

In terms of investment in teacher and educational staff development, we find:

•Professional training and continuous development: The UAE offers ongoing training programs for teachers and educational staff to develop their skills and benefit from the latest educational curricula.

•Promoting excellence and innovation in education: The UAE encourages excellence and innovation in education by offering rewards and financial support to creative schools and teachers.

•Career guidance and career paths: The UAE focuses on providing career guidance for students and offering job opportunities and field training in various industries.

Regarding the national education strategy, the UAE adopts ambitious national educational strategies to enhance human capabilities and develop the community. These strategies include improving the educational environment and promoting innovation and scientific research in the educational field.

The developments in the educational sector in the UAE reflect its serious commitment to providing high-quality, advanced education that contributes to sustainable progress and prosperity. Efforts continue to develop infrastructure and modern educational facilities to meet the aspirations of the community and the growing needs of the labor market.

Technological Infrastructure and Telecommunications

In the UAE, technological infrastructure and telecommunications are fundamental components of modern infrastructure transformations, serving as the backbone for economic and social development. The UAE is distinguished by its adoption of the latest technologies and modern facilities to ensure an ideal environment for living, working, and innovation.

Regarding the transformations and improvements in technological infrastructure and telecommunications, we observe:

•Advanced digital infrastructure: The UAE invests heavily in developing its digital infrastructure, including high-speed internet networks (5G). This investment ensures fast and reliable communications for citizens and residents.

•Smart applications and solutions: The UAE encourages the use of artificial intelligence applications and smart solutions in various sectors, such as healthcare, education, and smart government. This aims to improve efficiency and provide better services to the community.

•Technology in the healthcare and education sectors: The integration of technology is an integral part of enhancing vital sectors like healthcare and education. The UAE offers advanced technological solutions in these fields to enhance services and improve quality.

•Innovation and investment in technology companies: The UAE supports innovation and investment in emerging technology companies, boosting the landscape of innovation and entrepreneurship in the country.

Regarding future vision and strategies, the UAE adopts an ambitious vision to become one of the most technologically advanced countries in the world. The UAE government is developing long-term strategies to promote innovation and leverage technology to enhance government services and improve the quality of life.

The UAE is a leading nation in the field of technological infrastructure and telecommunications, continuing its substantial investments to achieve development and innovation in these critical sectors. This modern infrastructure plays a crucial role in supporting economic growth and promoting sustainable development in the UAE.

Challenges of Urban Renaissance and Future Prospects

Challenges of Urban Renaissance

In the UAE, architectural and planning challenges are evolving and transforming significantly due to rapid growth and continuous development across various economic and social sectors. Urban planners and engineers in the UAE face diverse and complex challenges, yet they are creative in finding innovative solutions to achieve sustainable development and fulfill the country's vision for the future. Some of the key challenges of urban renaissance in the UAE include:

•Rapid growth and urban development: The UAE is one of the fastest-growing countries in the world, which puts pressure on urban planning and necessitates effective solutions to manage rapid urban growth.

•Environmental sustainability: The UAE strives to balance urban development with environmental sustainability, requiring the adoption of architectural and planning designs that use energy efficiently and reduce environmental pollution.

•Cultural and community diversity: The UAE's society is characterized by its cultural and demographic diversity, necessitating infrastructure planning that meets the needs and aspirations of various segments of the community.

•Technology and innovation: Continuous advancements in technology and innovation demand integration and interaction between architectural design and urban planning to incorporate the latest technologies in city and building development.

•Diversification of communities and facilities: Future planning requires diversification in the provision of public and recreational facilities to meet the needs of various community segments, reflecting cultural and demographic diversity.

•Innovation in architectural design: The UAE encourages innovation in architectural design by organizing competitions and exhibitions to inspire engineers and designers to present new and sustainable ideas.

•International cooperation and partnerships: The UAE benefits from international cooperation and partnerships with global entities in the field of planning and infrastructure, contributing to the transfer of best practices and global experiences to the country.

Future Prospects of Urban Renaissance

The United Arab Emirates is moving towards a bright future and an inspiring urban renaissance that transcends current challenges and outlines promising future horizons in urban development and infrastructure. The UAE is an exemplary model in achieving progress and sustainable development on a global level, continuing to take bold steps towards enhancing the quality of life and the well-being of society.

The prospects of the urban renaissance in the UAE are based on Vision 2071, which aims to make the UAE one of the best countries in the world by the year 2071. This vision focuses on developing infrastructure, innovation, and building an advanced and sustainable society. A summary of some of the prospects of the urban renaissance in the UAE is as follows:

• Smart and Sustainable Cities: The UAE has adopted an advanced vision for building smart cities that rely on technology and innovation to improve the quality of life. These cities aim to achieve environmental, economic, and social sustainability, providing an urban environment characterized by efficiency and comfort for residents.

• Advanced Public Transportation: The UAE strives to improve and develop public transportation systems and promote environmentally friendly modes of transport, contributing to reduced traffic congestion and improved air quality.

• Environmental Sustainability and Clean Energy: The UAE seeks to enhance the use of renewable energy and apply green building principles in urban projects, aiming to reduce the environmental footprint and preserve natural resources.

• Technology and Innovation in Urban Design: Technology and innovation form an essential part of future infrastructure development, integrating innovative technological solutions into the design of cities and buildings to achieve efficiency and flexibility.

The prospects of the urban renaissance in the UAE are impressive, focusing on achieving sustainable development and prosperity for society. The UAE continues its journey towards realizing a bright future vision through innovation and investment in urban infrastructure and technology.

With a balance between architectural and planning challenges, prospects, and initiatives, the UAE aspires to achieve its vision of being a global center for innovation and sustainable development. Efforts continue in this field to ensure the development of a sustainable architectural and urban environment that meets the needs and aspirations of society and enhances sustainable development in the long term.

Chapter 7

The Human Renaissance

The human renaissance in the United Arab Emirates constitutes an essential part of its journey towards progress and sustainable development. The UAE serves as a vivid example of achieving comprehensive advancement through substantial investments in education, healthcare, and infrastructure, with a focus on human development as the cornerstone for growth and evolution.

Education and Human Development

The United Arab Emirates is a global leader in education and human development, viewing human renaissance as a vital part of its future vision to build an advanced and innovative knowledge-based society. The educational system in the UAE is distinguished by its focus on the comprehensive development of individuals through advanced and innovative educational programs.

The UAE is one of the most advanced Arab countries in education and human development, with the government adopting innovative educational strategies aimed at developing individual skills and fostering creativity and innovation. The educational system emphasizes providing exceptional educational opportunities for all segments of society.

In the field of higher education and scientific research within the framework of human renaissance, the UAE pays great attention to the development of higher education and scientific research. The government invests significantly in educational institutions and universities and encourages partnerships with the best universities and research centers globally. For example, the Mohammed Bin Rashid Center for Government Innovation and Registration (MBRISC) is a leader in this field.

In the realm of educational technology and remote learning, the UAE's educational sector has witnessed a revolution in the use of technology to enhance the learning experience. Remote learning strategies are now an integral part of the educational approach, especially during the pandemic, which pushed many educational institutions to intensively develop online learning methods.

In addition to skill development and continuous training, the UAE is a hub for skill development and continuous training, with numerous programs and training courses supported across various fields. The government and the private sector encourage providing learning opportunities and developing work skills within the community.

Healthcare

Healthcare in the United Arab Emirates is a vital element in the human renaissance and the realization of the civilizational miracle the country has witnessed over the past few decades. This renaissance has been represented by a comprehensive development in the healthcare sector, contributing to improved quality of life and societal well-being.

A key aspect of this healthcare revolution in the UAE is the wise and pioneering vision of the political leadership, which has made health one of its top priorities. The healthcare infrastructure has been significantly developed, with the establishment of modern hospitals, advanced medical centers, and distinguished health facilities. This includes the creation of integrated medical centers and specialized hospitals that provide high-quality services to citizens and residents.

In addition to infrastructure improvements, there has been a focus on developing human skills in healthcare by enhancing medical education and training medical personnel. The latest medical and scientific technologies have also been employed in treatment and diagnosis, contributing to the high level of healthcare provided.

The approach in the UAE is comprehensive, offering health services to all social and professional groups, including maternity and child care, urgent care, and elderly care. There has also been an emphasis on health awareness and disease prevention, which has improved public health.

The success of healthcare in the UAE represents a model of civilizational renaissance, with substantial investments in this field being a well-thought-out strategy to achieve progress and development in various aspects of human life. Thanks to these efforts, the UAE has achieved a comprehensive renaissance in healthcare, making it a role model in the field of healthcare at the international level.

Development of Education and Scientific Research

Scientific research in the United Arab Emirates represents a vital part of the human renaissance and the civilizational miracle that the country has experienced in recent decades. This renaissance signifies a comprehensive transformation in the scientific and research field, positioning the UAE as a hub for innovation and development across various scientific and technological domains.

The wise leadership in the UAE has significantly bolstered scientific research by adopting policies and strategies aimed at promoting innovation and supporting the sciences. Advanced research centers and prestigious universities have been established, providing a rich environment filled with opportunities for local and international researchers and scientists to work and innovate.

Among the most notable fields that have seen tremendous progress in the UAE are information and communication technology, renewable energy, biomedical sciences, space and astronomy, and engineering and technological innovation. Significant investments have been allocated to support research and development in these areas, leading to increased scientific and technical productivity and tangible advancements.

The UAE strives for excellence in scientific research by encouraging international cooperation and the exchange of expertise with renowned global research centers and universities. The state pays special attention to developing human talents in scientific fields through advanced educational and training programs that contribute to building a generation of creative and innovative researchers.

Scientific research in the UAE is considered a key factor in enhancing the civilizational renaissance the country has experienced, contributing to innovation, and sustainability, and steering the future towards a more advanced and developed knowledge-based society.

The Role of Youth in the UAE's Civilizational Renaissance

The role of youth in the UAE's civilizational renaissance is a vital and decisive element in the country's journey towards progress and prosperity. Over the past few years, the UAE has witnessed significant social and economic transformations that have empowered young people and harnessed their energies across various fields. The pivotal role of youth is one of the crucial factors that have contributed to the UAE's civilizational miracle.

Youth in the UAE are a primary driver of change and innovation. Significant support has been provided to the youth through advanced educational and training programs aimed at developing their skills and leveraging their creativity in vital areas such as technology, innovation, entrepreneurship, and culture.

Furthermore, the UAE government works to empower youth and encourage their active participation in developing the national economy, where the youth are considered key partners in building the state's future and achieving the UAE Vision 2071, which aims to make the UAE one of the best countries in the world.

The role of youth in the UAE's civilizational renaissance stands out as a true catalyst for social and economic transformation, emphasizing the activation of human potential and the achievement of sustainable development.

The Prominence of Emirati Women as a Pillar of the Nation's Renaissance

The United Arab Emirates shines as one of the world's leading destinations, proudly and creatively carrying the banner of progress and cultural advancement. It's remarkable journey over recent decades reveals significant transformations, driven by collective effort and notable government dedication. At the heart of this comprehensive renaissance stands the vital role of Emirati women, whose impactful contributions cannot be overlooked in this bright cultural trajectory.

Emirati women have begun to take on more active roles across various fields, including political, economic, and social leadership. Their role has been bolstered by supportive and encouraging government policies aimed at empowering women and providing equal opportunities in education, employment, and political participation. The UAE has positioned itself as a global model in achieving gender equality and supporting women's advancement in all fields.

Emirati women play a crucial and vital role in shaping the state's cultural renaissance, serving as a fundamental element and a strong pillar in building society and achieving comprehensive progress. Women are not merely partners in society; they represent a driving force and a symbol of excellence and brilliance across various essential sectors of national life.

The participation of Emirati women in various vital fields is evident, as they actively and fruitfully contribute to the development of the state's economic, social, and cultural infrastructure. This is achieved through their representation in various councils, institutions, and national companies, striving for the civilizational renaissance of the state.

One of the most prominent factors contributing to women's empowerment in the UAE is the educational renaissance. The state has witnessed significant advancements in the education sector, where education forms a cornerstone for women's development and excellence in various domains. Thanks to the UAE government's relentless efforts to provide free, high-quality education for all and exceptional educational opportunities for both genders, Emirati women have become an integral part of the distinguished education system in the country. They strive to disseminate knowledge and enhance overall educational standards, excelling in their journey towards progress. Through the government's notable focus on their education, Emirati women have acquired the necessary skills and knowledge for effective participation in building and developing society.

Emirati women hold leadership positions in government and politics in the UAE, enjoying equal opportunities and rights with men to participate in decision-making, legislation, and shaping the national future. They are active partners in political life, and thanks to female representation in the Federal National Council, they can effectively contribute to directing and developing national policies, reflecting the state's progress and enhancing community participation. The presence of women in the political scene positively influences society, where they are seen as leaders of positive change.

Women play a significant role in the UAE labor market, working diligently and with dedication across various economic sectors, holding leadership positions, and enjoying equal opportunities for employment and career advancement. Emirati women are among the most active and creative segments in different economic sectors, from industry to financial services. Thanks to their entrepreneurial spirit and creativity, many women own successful businesses, contributing to national economic growth, achieving sustainable development, and enhancing the UAE's international standing.

Emirati women are an integral part of the country's cultural and social life, striving to balance professional and family life, making them active partners in the development of social sectors. They contribute effectively through their participation in cultural and artistic events, enhancing social communication and understanding among community members. They play a significant role in developing social sectors such as education, health, and culture.

The UAE government provides a supportive and encouraging environment for empowering women and enhancing their active role in society by launching various strategies and initiatives to encourage female participation in vital national fields.

The contributions of Emirati women exemplify excellence and creativity in the state's cultural renaissance journey. They are a fundamental element in building a prosperous future, a vital pillar in the path towards development and progress, and indispensable partners in achieving sustainable development goals and the comprehensive well-being of Emirati society.

The Impact of Cultural Renaissance
on Emirati Society

The impact of the cultural renaissance on Emirati society represents an inspiring success story of social, economic, and cultural transformation that the UAE has witnessed over recent decades. This renaissance was not merely economic progress but a comprehensive shift in the lives of the people and their communities.

One of the most notable effects of the cultural renaissance is the tangible economic transformation that has led to improved living standards, increased job opportunities, and overall development. The UAE has become a global economic and financial hub, attracting investments and talents from around the world, thereby enhancing employment opportunities and improving the community's living standards.

Moreover, human development is one of the key aspects of the cultural renaissance, with comprehensive and outstanding provision of education and healthcare. The UAE has succeeded in building a high-level educational infrastructure, including advanced universities and prestigious research centers, which have contributed to qualifying the youth and developing their skills and capabilities.

Culturally and socially, the cultural renaissance has promoted tolerance, diversity, and cultural interaction among the various cultures and nationalities living in the UAE. Today, Emirati society is considered one of the most diverse and open communities in the region.

Overall, the impact of the cultural renaissance on Emirati society represents a revival of national identity and pride, strengthening national unity and belonging. This cultural transformation reflects a successful strategy for achieving sustainable development and realizing an ambitious future vision.

Chapter 8

Electronic Government

The Concept of E-Government and Its Importance in the Modern Era

In light of the rapid technological development we have witnessed in recent decades, e-government has become one of the most important concepts embodying that digital revolution. E-government is a modern model for state management that primarily relies on the application of information and communication technologies to government functions and procedures to increase efficiency and transparency. It enhances citizen participation and improves and accelerates operations, increasing the quality of public services. This modern concept is a practical application of the "smart government" model, aiming to achieve sustainable development and well-being for citizens through the use of technology and the improvement of public service performance. The importance of e-government in the modern era can be demonstrated through:

Improving the Quality of Government Services

Electronic government contributes to enhancing the quality and speed of government services provided to citizens and residents. Through websites and smart applications, these services can be easily accessed online anytime, anywhere without the need to visit official government entities. Electronic services also enable direct submission of requests and transactions without complications, saving time and effort for citizens.

Enhancing Transparency and Accountability

Electronic government serves as a powerful tool for enhancing transparency and accountability in governmental work. By transparently publishing government information and official decisions online, readily accessible to everyone, citizens and residents can easily access information, increasing trust in the government and promoting transparency in public affairs management. It gives individuals the opportunity for effective participation in the decision-making process.

Improving Government Productivity and Efficiency

Electronic government contributes by providing a work environment that allows employees to improve their performance and relieve them of routine tasks. Thanks to the use of technology and electronic systems, employees can accomplish their tasks more efficiently and quickly, allowing them more time and effort to focus on high-priority tasks and creative thinking. Consequently, productivity is enhanced, and government performance in serving citizens and meeting their needs is improved better and faster.

Cost Savings and Increased Efficiency

Electronic government contributes to reducing administrative costs and increasing government work efficiency by reducing costs associated with printing, paper, and storage, and improving administrative processes through electronic organization and advanced technology.

Saving Time and Effort

Through electronic government, citizens can complete many procedures and transactions quickly and efficiently without the need to wait in queues or submit paper documents. This saves time and effort for citizens and contributes to improving their quality of life.

Enhancing Participation and Social Interaction

Electronic government encourages social interaction and participation, allowing citizens to express their opinions and suggestions through social media platforms and official government websites. This creates a participatory environment that enhances communication between the government and citizens and contributes to improving services and meeting the needs of the community.

Achieving Sustainable Development

Electronic government is a vital tool for achieving sustainable development, contributing to the development of technological infrastructure, and enhancing the state's capacity to provide basic services to citizens effectively.

Electronic government is a modern and important concept and a vital tool in developing government administration and improving citizen services in the modern age, contributing to the development and improvement of various communities. By using technology and innovation in public affairs management, countries can achieve significant benefits and improve the quality of life for their citizens tangibly and meet their needs more effectively.

Stages of Evolution of E-Government in the UAE

The United Arab Emirates (UAE) is among the leading countries in adopting technology and its applications in various aspects of life, including the government sector. E-government is an essential part of the UAE's vision for achieving excellence and innovation in providing services to citizens and residents. Through its strategic vision and continuous investments in technology, the UAE has established a leading position globally in e-government. This development was not coincidental but the result of a long journey of meticulous planning and execution.

Historically, efforts to build e-government in the UAE began in the early 21st century. In 2000, Sheikh Mohammed bin Rashid Al Maktoum launched the "e-Government" program, laying the foundation for the digital transformation journey in the UAE. This pioneering step reflected a clear futuristic vision, as government institutions began to transform their traditional services into innovative electronic services available online 24/7, aimed at facilitating and enhancing the experience of citizens and residents. Early developments in adopting modern technology improved government procedures and accessibility, with e-government systems implemented in various fields such as education, healthcare, finance, environment, and more.

In 2013, the transition to smart government occurred as the UAE entered a new phase with the launch of the Smart Government initiative, marking a qualitative leap from e-government to smart government. The country successfully achieved a complete smart transformation of its services, which had a positive impact on investors and citizens alike.

In recent years, the UAE has witnessed a comprehensive digital transformation in various aspects of government life. Advanced technologies such as artificial intelligence, big data analytics, encryption, and cloud computing have been implemented to enhance the efficiency of government services and improve user experience.

The UAE launched the UAE Vision 2021 and UAE Vision 2031 projects, aiming to enhance and transform the government sector into a global leading model. The UAE topped the region in digital transformation rankings, thanks to its continuous strategies and initiatives. The country maintained its position as the top Arab country and jumped to the 13th position globally in the E-Government Development Index for 2022.

Among the key aspects focused on in the evolution of e-government in the UAE is improving user experience, with electronic government services designed to be easily accessible and user-friendly for all segments of society.

The UAE looks forward to further development in e-government, seeking to utilize the latest technologies such as virtual reality and augmented reality to enhance user interaction with government services.

To achieve this advancement, the UAE relies on partnerships with the private sector and investments in technological infrastructure, in addition to developing human capabilities through training and development.

The evolution of e-government in the UAE is an excellent example of the effective use of technology to improve government services and enhance interaction between citizens and the government. With the UAE's commitment to innovation and continuous development, more improvements and advancements in this field can be expected in the future.

The UAE continues to enhance its position as a global model for digital transformation, focusing on sustainability and shaping the future. The country represents an ideal environment for economic and commercial activities, providing a comprehensive smart experience for citizens and residents.

Vision and Core Pillars of Digital Transformation in the UAE

Digital transformation in the UAE is a comprehensive journey aimed at converting traditional services and processes into advanced digital systems, to enhance the efficiency of both government and private sector performance and improve individuals' quality of life. This transformation is a fundamental cornerstone for achieving sustainable development and leadership in various fields. The UAE adopts a strategic vision for digital transformation based on several core pillars, including:

• Smart Government: The UAE aspires to build a smart government that delivers its services with high efficiency and uses the latest technologies through digital channels. This approach aims to facilitate access to government services for citizens and residents, thereby improving their experience and saving time and effort.

• Digital Infrastructure: The UAE has adopted the development of a robust digital infrastructure to support communications and information technology and enhance the use of digital services. This strong focus on digital infrastructure is in response to the growing societal need for information and communication technology and to ensure the provision of an advanced digital environment that supports innovation and development across various sectors.

• Innovation and Artificial Intelligence: The UAE continues to enhance its support for innovation and the use of advanced technologies such as artificial intelligence in various sectors, aiming to improve service quality and provide innovative solutions that meet society's needs.

• Cybersecurity: Cybersecurity is an integral part of the digital transformation journey, where the UAE places great importance on enhancing electronic security to protect data and ensure privacy. The main challenge lies in developing advanced strategies and adopting modern technical tools to counter increasing cyber threats and ensure the continuity of digital operations safely and confidently.

• E-commerce: The UAE witnessed significant growth in the e-commerce sector, reflecting the digital transformation that affects purchasing behavior and financial transactions. Consumers and businesses widely rely on the Internet to make purchases and complete commercial transactions, reflecting a gradual transition towards using digital means to achieve business objectives and meet market needs more effectively and efficiently.

• Digital Education and Training: The UAE greatly emphasizes developing digital skills for individuals through education and training programs, aiming to enable them to effectively participate in the digital economy. These efforts are an essential part of the state's strategy to enhance individual capabilities and enable them to keep pace with modern technological advancements, developing the necessary skills to capitalize on opportunities available in the digital age.

• Digital Inclusion: The UAE strives to ensure fair and equal access for all segments of society to digital services, aiming to achieve the principle of digital inclusion. This effort reflects the state's commitment to providing equal opportunities for everyone to benefit from modern technologies and enjoy the advantages of the digital age without discrimination or bias.

Furthermore, the UAE places significant emphasis on enhancing communication and interaction with citizens and residents through providing digital platforms for submitting complaints, suggestions, and feedback, and enhancing electronic interaction with various segments of society.

In the context of innovation and entrepreneurship, the UAE encourages innovation in technology and digital creativity by supporting startups, providing support and funding for innovators and creators, and organizing events and competitions to encourage innovation and the exchange of ideas and experiences.

These core pillars are part of a comprehensive strategy aimed at achieving full digital transformation in the

UAE, which is a part of the Fourth Industrial Revolution that fundamentally relies on technology and innovation. The UAE continues to enhance its position as a leading country in digital transformation globally, through adopting the latest technologies and smart solutions that contribute to accelerating the pace of transformation and improving the quality of life for individuals.

Digital transformation in the UAE is a vital part of the state's vision to achieve sustainable development and leadership in the digital age. Legal frameworks and institutional regulations play a fundamental role in supporting and enhancing this transformation and securing the necessary legal and regulatory infrastructure to ensure the effective and secure operation of digital processes.

The UAE is among the leading countries in establishing legal frameworks and supportive regulations for e-government. Specialized legal entities and structures have been established to develop and enhance the legal environment supporting digital transformation, such as the Dubai Government's Electronic Development Center and the Abu Dhabi Center for Technical Arbitration.

In addition, the institutional regulations supporting e-government include several laws and regulations covering various legal and regulatory aspects related to technology, information, and communications, such as the Personal Data Protection Law, Cybercrime Law, Cybersecurity Law, and others. These laws aim to protect personal data, combat cybercrime, enhance cybersecurity, and promote secure and trusted electronic exchange.

Furthermore, the UAE adopts a comprehensive strategy to enhance transparency and accountability in e-government work, through legislation that enables public access to information and promotes a culture of transparency and accountability. By relying on this supportive legal framework and institutional regulations, the UAE continues to enhance its position as a leading center for digital transformation, providing a favorable legislative and legal environment for investment and innovation in technology and digital creativity.

The Digital Infrastructure in the UAE

The digital infrastructure in the United Arab Emirates (UAE) is considered one of the key foundations for achieving digital transformation and enhancing the country's status as a global hub for innovation and technology. This infrastructure encompasses a wide range of technological elements and networks that contribute to accelerating development and improving the quality of life for citizens and residents.

The digital infrastructure in the UAE is the backbone of the digital transformation witnessed by the country, representing the foundation upon which digital services are provided and innovation is achieved across various sectors.

The UAE has made significant progress in the EGDI index, ranking first globally in 2020. This progress is attributed to continuous efforts to develop digital infrastructure, improve e-government services, and enhance digital skills among citizens.

The technological infrastructure and networks include a range of vital elements that support secure and efficient communication and data transmission, including:

• **Technological Infrastructure**: The UAE is a leading country in investing in building technological infrastructure, with the government injecting massive investments into developing networks and improving digital infrastructure. These investments include developing fast internet networks and providing advanced communication services, including 5G wireless communication technologies.

The technological infrastructure in the UAE is characterized by development and diversity, incorporating advanced data centers, cloud computing technologies, and advanced cybersecurity systems. These elements are essential for providing efficient and secure digital government services and meeting the evolving and innovative needs of citizens and residents.

Advanced data centers in the UAE provide a strong foundation for data storage and processing, helping to provide stable and reliable digital services. Advanced cloud computing technologies play a crucial role in enabling the government to provide digital services with high efficiency and low cost, enhancing economic and social development in the country.

Thanks to these integrated and advanced elements in the technological infrastructure, individuals and institutions in the UAE can enjoy distinguished digital government services that promote effective communication and interaction and achieve high levels of digital security and safety. Cybersecurity systems work to protect sensitive data and information from electronic threats, ensuring the digital environment's safety for citizens and institutions.

The UAE continues to invest in developing and improving technological infrastructure, enhancing its position as a major center for technology and innovation in the region and globally.

• **Networks**: The UAE benefits from an advanced communication network that ensures the availability of digital services effectively. This network includes fiber optics and 5G technologies. This technological diversity is a vital foundation for providing high-speed internet and comprehensive coverage, supporting digital services, and smart applications, and contributing to enhancing effective interaction and communication between individuals and institutions.

• **Continuous Development**: The UAE continues its efforts to develop its digital infrastructure through significant investments in modern technology, such as the Internet of Things (IoT) and Artificial Intelligence (AI). This aims to enhance its capabilities in providing smart government services and building smart cities, contributing to enhancing interaction and communication between the government and citizens more effectively.

• **Government Collaboration**: The Telecommunications and Digital Government Regulatory Authority (TDRA) plays a vital role in providing and supporting digital infrastructure and developing the necessary strategies to drive digital transformation at the state level. TDRA's responsibilities include providing the necessary infrastructure to support e-government applications and digital services, including regulating and managing the use of digital technology efficiently and effectively. These efforts aim to enhance electronic interaction between the government and citizens, achieving comprehensive digital transformation in various vital sectors and areas.

• **Digital Empowerment**: The Government Empowerment Department in the Emirate of Abu Dhabi seeks to lead the digital future, adopting a pioneering vision to achieve comprehensive and effective digital transformation. In contrast, the Dubai Digital Authority is responsible for leadership in information technology, data, smart, and digital transformation, and works on developing and implementing the necessary strategies and initiatives to achieve the emirate's goals in this field. In this way, the two entities cooperate in building a sustainable and prosperous digital future for both Emirates, with continuous guidance towards progress and innovation in the digital age.

• **Sustainability and Innovation**: The UAE attaches great importance to establishing the foundations of sustainability as an essential part of its technological development journey. The country works on formulating clear strategies and plans aimed at ensuring the prosperity of the digital economy by directing its efforts towards maximizing the benefits of technology in a sustainable and environmentally friendly manner. These efforts play a vital role in enhancing sustainable economic growth and achieving sustainable development in various sectors and fields, contributing to enhancing the UAE's position as a global center for innovation and technological leadership.

Through these efforts, the United Arab Emirates demonstrates a strong commitment to developing an advanced and secure digital environment that contributes to achieving societal well-being and sustainable development. Through continuous investment in digital infrastructure, the UAE enhances its position as a global center for innovation and excellence in digital services.

Cybersecurity and Information Protection

Cybersecurity and information protection are of paramount importance to the United Arab Emirates (UAE), given the rapid technological advancements and comprehensive digital transformation witnessed by the country.

The significance of cybersecurity lies in protecting the digital assets of the state, including sensitive government information and personal data of citizens and residents. The UAE aims to enhance trust in technology use, stimulate innovation, and boost e-commerce by providing a secure and reliable digital environment.

The UAE adopts a multidimensional strategy for cybersecurity, including collaboration with the private and international sectors, developing national cybersecurity capabilities, and providing necessary legislation and regulations to enhance the legal protection of data and information.

Government entities and private institutions in the UAE implement best practices in cybersecurity, such as implementing preventive, responsive, and recovery measures against cyber-attacks, and enhancing awareness and training in this regard.

Moreover, the UAE experiences continuous development in the cybersecurity sector through investments in modern technologies such as artificial intelligence and big data analytics to enhance rapid response capabilities to threats and cyber attacks.

Given that cybersecurity and information protection are integral priorities for the UAE government, the state supports the development and implementation of comprehensive cybersecurity strategies to protect its data and information technology from growing electronic threats. The UAE takes a series of strategic and legislative measures to ensure the safety of the digital space and the protection of data and information.

Legislative and Legal Framework

Several laws and regulations have been developed to enhance cybersecurity, such as:

• The Anti-Rumor and Cybercrime Law, which aims to provide a legal framework to protect society from cybercrimes.

• The Guidance Document, representing the "Information Security Assurance System in the UAE," which provides a reference for the requirements of protecting information security assets.

Initiatives and Programs

• The Razzam Cybersecurity App, which utilizes advanced analytical techniques and artificial intelligence algorithms to identify malicious sites and ensure safe browsing. Serving all segments of society comprehensively, the "Razzam" app benefits from AI, machine learning, and big data analytics to enhance its continuous recognition of unsafe sites. The app sends visual alerts and automatically blocks harmful sites, aiming to provide a safe and reliable browsing experience in the future, making it one of the leading practical applications in the field of electronic protection.

• The Federal Network (FEDNET) provides a multi-layered secure environment and ensures the highest levels of security in the infrastructure.

• The "Cyber Pulse" initiative aims to disseminate cybersecurity culture and enhance the participation of all members of society.

• The aeCERT (National Computer Emergency Response Center) works to improve information security standards and practices.

Authorities and Councils

• The Cybersecurity Council proposes and prepares the necessary legislation, policies, and standards to enhance cybersecurity.

• The Telecommunications and Digital Government Regulatory Authority launches initiatives and guidelines to enhance a secure digital environment.

In terms of international cooperation, the UAE works to enhance international cooperation in the field of cybersecurity to address cross-border threats and exchange experiences and best practices.

The UAE attaches great importance to raising awareness among citizens and residents about the importance of cybersecurity and offers training courses and workshops to raise awareness and knowledge in this field.

Through these efforts, the UAE seeks to achieve a safe and reliable digital environment that protects individuals and institutions from cyber risks and ensures the continuity of digital business and services efficiently and securely.

The UAE's ongoing commitment to cybersecurity and information protection reflects its readiness to face modern digital challenges and achieve a prosperous and reliable future vision.

Technical and Security Challenges of E-Government in the UAE

The e-government in the United Arab Emirates faces multiple technical and security challenges that require integrated strategies for effective management. These challenges are a vital part of developing the digital infrastructure and enhancing cybersecurity within the Emirati community. Some of these challenges and how to address them can be outlined as follows:

Cyber Attacks and Cybersecurity

The e-government in the United Arab Emirates (UAE) is witnessing a continuous increase in the number and complexity of advanced cyber attacks. Hackers and attackers aim to target government data and critical infrastructure to disrupt services and cause widespread chaos. To address this challenge, the government takes multiple measures, including enhancing cybersecurity, improving awareness of electronic security, and developing technical capabilities to counter attacks.

Digital Transformation and Adoption of New Technologies

The United Arab Emirates is undergoing a significant digital transformation across government sectors, relying on information and communication technology to enhance government services and achieve citizen and resident satisfaction. This transformation is part of the UAE Vision 2071, which aims to make the UAE one of the most advanced countries economically and socially.

The e-government is experiencing a continuous digital transformation that requires continuous reliance on new technologies such as artificial intelligence, cloud computing, smart internet, and big data analytics. This transformation requires significant investments in training and technological updates to ensure full utilization of the benefits of these technologies and to ensure the availability of the necessary infrastructure to operate them efficiently.

Digital transformation in the UAE is considered a vital path towards an advanced and prosperous future, where the government will continue to invest in technology to enhance innovation and achieve excellence in delivering government services. It is expected that the future will witness further developments in areas such as artificial intelligence and big data analytics, enhancing the UAE's position as a global leader in digital transformation.

The strategic vision of the UAE focuses on developing e-government sectors to improve the efficiency of government services and achieve excellence and innovation in service delivery to citizens and residents. This vision has included the launch of several digital initiatives and programs such as "Smart Dubai" and "Emirati Digital Transformation" with the aim of providing integrated and easy government services to citizens.

The UAE government is striving to enhance digital transformation through investment in information and communication technology. Many government sectors have witnessed successful and innovative applications of digital transformation, such as the electronic health system and smart police system, leading to improved efficiency and better services for citizens.

Despite significant achievements, the UAE government faces numerous challenges in its journey towards digital transformation, such as security and privacy challenges and adopting modern technology. However, with these challenges come significant opportunities to enhance international cooperation and exchange expertise in digital transformation.

Privacy and Data Protection

Data protection and ensuring privacy are of utmost importance in the digital environment. This requires implementing strict measures to protect personal and sensitive data and ensuring compliance with legislation and regulations related to data protection, such as the Personal Data Protection Law in the UAE.

Compliance with International Standards and Legislation

The e-government in the UAE faces challenges in complying with international standards and local and international legislation related to technology and cybersecurity. This requires the development of a legal and regulatory framework that ensures full compliance and transparency in all electronic operations.

Addressing these challenges requires cooperation and integration between the public and private sectors, in addition to leveraging international expertise and knowledge in cybersecurity and digital technology. Through comprehensive and multi-dimensional strategies, the UAE government can successfully address these challenges and achieve its vision for a prosperous digital future.

The Social and Economic Impact of E-Government in the UAE

The social and economic impact of e-government in the United Arab Emirates is a significant topic deserving analysis and exploration. The UAE is among the leading countries in implementing technology in e-government, leading to a substantial transformation in how citizens and residents interact with government services and administrative processes.

The Social Impact of E-Government in the UAE

• Enhancement of Government Services: Enabling citizens to access government services online enhances the speed and ease of access to information and procedures. It also reduces bureaucracy and complexity in dealing with government entities. Citizens and residents in the UAE can access a variety of government services faster and easier online, saving time and effort.

• Promotion of Transparency and Community Participation: Empowering citizens to monitor and participate in government decisions fosters transparency. Additionally, disseminating information and data online increases the transparency of government operations.

• Improvement of Efficiency and Cost Savings: By reducing paper and physical document usage, e-government initiatives lower costs and improve efficiency. Moreover, enhancing resource management and planning through electronic systems contributes to efficiency improvements.

• Encouragement of Innovation and Technological Advancement: Encouraging innovation in delivering government services online and developing new technologies enhances user experience and achieves digital transformation.

The Economic Impact of E-Government in the UAE:

• Enhancing Investment and Business: E-government initiatives improve the business environment by facilitating digital government procedures. Moreover, they attract investors by providing electronic platforms for trade and investment. The robust digital infrastructure and e-government enhance the UAE's reputation as an attractive destination for foreign investment, thus promoting the digital economy and contributing to business growth and innovation.

• Boosting Efficiency and Effectiveness: E-government implementation leads to improved administrative efficiency and cost reduction. Reducing reliance on traditional processes helps enhance productivity and achieve savings from an economic standpoint.

• Improving Government Revenues: Advanced electronic systems enhance tax collection and fee payment, thus contributing to improved government revenues. Additionally, providing electronic financial services contributes to financial returns.

• Providing Employment Opportunities and Skill Development: Stimulating the technology sector and providing jobs in software development and information technology contribute to job creation and skill development. Moreover, developing training programs to qualify national cadres in the field of technology enhances human capital.

• Fostering Innovation and Entrepreneurship: E-government promotes an environment of innovation and entrepreneurship by supporting technology companies and investing in future technologies.

The implementation of e-government in the UAE represents a strategic investment that enhances social interaction and brings about an economic transformation in the economic infrastructure. This transition requires sustained efforts to enhance technological infrastructure and improve communication between the government and citizens to ensure the continued realization of the social and economic benefits resulting from this advanced digital strategy.

The Civilizational Impact of E-Government in the UAE

The role of e-government in the UAE is characterized by the comprehensive application of information and communication technology to achieve civilizational advancement on multiple levels:

• Development of Technological Infrastructure: The UAE is a leading country in building modern technological infrastructure. The government has invested in developing high-speed internet and communication networks and constructing advanced data centers, facilitating the effective and seamless delivery of its services online.

• Enhancement of Government Services: The UAE government seeks to improve the quality of government services through the transition to e-government. Citizens and residents can easily access their government transactions through smartphones or computers, saving time and effort.

• Promotion of Transparency and Anti-Corruption: E-government is an effective means to promote transparency and combat corruption. With transparent electronic systems in place, citizens can monitor government transactions and better oversee the performance of government entities.

• Stimulating Innovation and Entrepreneurship:
The UAE government encourages innovation and
entrepreneurship by supporting technological
projects and startups. Financial and technical
support is provided to innovators and
entrepreneurs to transform creative ideas into
successful projects.

• Improvement of Work Environment and Digital
Economy: E-government enhances the work
environment and digital economy by providing
the necessary infrastructure and support to
technology companies and digital businesses.

The e-government in the UAE serves as a strong
driver for civilizational advancement by
supporting technology and innovation, improving
government services, promoting transparency
and combating corruption, and contributing to
comprehensive development and prosperity in
society.

Arabic and foreign references

1-" .History of the Emirates," Comprehensive Emirates Encyclopedia.
2-" .The Emirates... History of Greatness and Development," book by Abdullah Al Mansoori.
3-" .From Emirates' Origins to Its Culture Today," article in Al Bayan Magazine.
4-" .The Emirates... Center of Civilization and Development," website of Union Printing and Publishing.
 5-"The Emirates... History of Unity and Development," Emirates Today Magazine.
6-" .History of the Emirates | Official Portal of the United Arab Emirates Government (u.ae)"
7-" .History of the Emirates: Journey from Antiquity to the Present," Department of Culture and Tourism in the Emirates.
8-" .History of the Emirates: Modern Era and Economic Prosperity," Emirates Center for Studies and Research.
9-" .Ancient History of the Emirates: Journey through the World of Sea and Desert," Official Emirates History Website.
10-" .Impact of Islamic Civilization on the Emirates," scientific article published in Journal of Islamic Studies.
11-" .The Emirates... From Poverty to Wealth," article in Emirates Economic Magazine.
12-" .Vision 2030 of the Emirates: Bright Future and Sustainable Development," article in Al Ittihad Emirates Newspaper.
13-" .Evolution of the Emirates: From Simplicity to Leadership," book by Mohammed Al Ramithi.
14-" .The Emirates: From Historical Memory to Gateway of the Future," Ministry of Culture website.
 15-".The Economic History of the United Arab Emirates," article in Emirates Economic Magazine.
 16-"Official Portal of the Emirates Government Provides a Comprehensive View of Emirates History".
17-The Emirates: A Global Peace Incubator and Supporter of Civilizational Dialogue," Gulf Newspaper (alkhaleej.ae).
18-State Annual Report for 2023," Ministry of Economic Development - United Arab Emirates.
19-Vision 2021 of the Emirates: Achieving Sustainable Development and Innovation," Government of the United Arab Emirates.
20-Establishment of the United Arab Emirates: History and Development," book by an academic in Emirati history.

21-" .Zayed bin Sultan Al Nahyan: Union Leader and State Builder," article in Emirates Historical Magazine.

22-" .Oil and Development in the United Arab Emirates," research article published in International Economics Journal.

23-The Seven Emirates | Official Portal of the United Arab Emirates Government (u.ae)"

24-" .The Emirates and Oil... 50-Year Journey of Challenges and Rapid Development" (al-ain.com).

25-" .Founder of the Emirates - Sheikh Zayed bin Sultan Al Nahyan" (mofa.gov.ae) 26.-UAE Innovation Strategy 2021-2031," Ministry of Economy - UAE.

27-" .National Advanced Innovation Strategy | Official Portal of the United Arab Emirates Government (u.ae)"

28-" .National Program for Small and Medium Enterprises Projects | Homepage (uaesme.ae)"

29-" .Official Portal of the United Arab Emirates Government (u.ae)"

30-" .National Innovation Strategies in the UAE (uaecabinet.ae)"

31-" .Innovation and Future Outlook | Official Portal of the United Arab Emirates Government (u.ae)"

32-" .Renewable Energy Strategy 2050," Ministry of Energy and Infrastructure, UAE.

33-" .Mohammed bin Rashid Solar Energy Project," Ministry of Energy and Infrastructure website.

34-UAE Economy Report," Ministry of Economy, 2023.

35-Sustainable Development in the UAE: Vision 2030," National Energy Management Authority, 2022.

36-" .Annual Report on Infrastructure in the Emirates," Emirates Development Foundation, 2022.

37-" .Vision 2071 of the Emirates: Enhancing Human Capabilities and Innovation," Office of the President, 2022.

38-" .Education and Development Strategy in the UAE: Vision 2030," Ministry of Education, 2021.

38-" .Technology and Innovation Strategy in the UAE: Vision 2030," Ministry of Technology and Innovation, 2021.

39-" .Innovation Report in the UAE," National Research Council, 2022.

40-" .Innovation and Competitiveness Report in the UAE," National Innovation Council, 2023.

41-" .Report: Education in the UAE Enhances the Comprehensive Civilization Renaissance Witnessed by the Country" (moe.gov.ae).

42-The UAE Solidifies Its Position in 'Infrastructure'... Fourth in the World in Competitiveness Report" (al-ain.com).

43-" .Economy of the UAE | Official Portal of the United Arab Emirates Government (u.ae)"

44-" .In the Foundations of the Emirati Renaissance | Kamal Al Hadi | Gulf Newspaper (alkhaleej.ae)"

45-" .Steps and Initiatives to Encourage Innovation | Official Portal of the United Arab Emirates Government (u.ae)"

46-" .Innovation | Official Portal of the United Arab Emirates Government (u.ae)"

47-" .Source City"... The Smart and Sustainable City of the Future (alwatanvoice.com)

48-" .Sustainable Smart Cities | Official Portal of the United Arab Emirates Government (u.ae)"

49-" .Technological Transformation Program | Official Portal of the United Arab Emirates Government (u.ae)"

50-" .Investment in Tourism | Ministry of Economy - United Arab Emirates (moec.gov.ae)"

51-" .Future Roadmap of the UAE | Official Portal of the United Arab Emirates Government (u.ae)"

52-" .UAE Vision 2071 | Official Portal of the United Arab Emirates Government (u.ae)"

53-" .Society and the 'We are the UAE 2031' Vision | Official Portal of the United Arab Emirates Government (u.ae)"

54-" .Future of Emirati Heritage | Abdullah Mohammed Al Sabab | Gulf Newspaper (alkhaleej.ae)"

55-" .Emirati Heritage: Features of the Present and Future | Gulf Newspaper (alkhaleej.ae)"

56-" .History of the Emirates: Gateway to the Past," Emirates Heritage Magazine, 2021.

57-" .The Emirates: Between Heritage and Modernity," National Authority for Tourism and Culture, 2020.

58-" .The Emirates: From Bedouin Roots to Burj Khalifa," book by Mohammed Al Ramithi.

59-" .The Emirates: Story of a Civilizational Renaissance," article in Emirates Today Magazine.

60-" .History of the Emirates: From Beginnings to Present," National Archives Center, 2021.

61-" .Emirates Throughout History: From the Desert to Prosperity," Ministry of Culture, Youth, and Community Development, 2018.

62-" .Development and Culture in the UAE: Paths of Balance and Harmony," Emirates Center for Studies and Research, 2019.

63-" .Emirati Heritage: Roots Embracing Modernity," Emirates Heritage and Culture Center, 2018.

64-" .History of the Emirates: From Beginnings to Present," National Archives Center, 2021.
65-" .Economic Evolution of the UAE: Journey from Oil to Diversity," Emirates Economic Magazine, 2019.
66-" .History of the Emirates: Journey from Simplicity to Leadership," Emirates History and Heritage Center, 2020.
67-" .Economic Transformations in the UAE: Analytical Study," National Statistics and Information Center, 2018.
68-" .The Emirates: Leadership and Comprehensive Development," Ministry of Economic Development, 2019.
69-" .History of the Emirates: Journey from Simplicity to Leadership," Emirates Development Magazine, 2020.
70-" .Development Strategies in the UAE: Realistic Vision," National Center for Studies and Research, 2019.
71-" .Journey of Economic Development in the UAE: Historical Study," Ministry of Planning and Development, 2018.
72-" .UAE Vision 2021: Plans and Strategies for Sustainable Development," National Statistics Authority, 2021.
73-Transformations in Education and Health Development in the UAE," Ministry of Education and Ministry of Health in the UAE, 2020.
74-" .UAE Vision 2071: Roadmap to the Future," Official Website of the UAE Government.
75-" .Enhancing the Innovation Environment in the UAE: Initiatives and Challenges," Emirates Institute for Studies and Research, 2021.

76-" .The UAE: Journey of Transformation and Development," Ministry of Culture, Youth, and Community Development, 2021.
77-" .The Story of the UAE: History and Modern Transformations," Emirates Historical Magazine, 2020.
78-" .History of the UAE: Volume One," Emirates Center for Studies and Research, 2018.
79-" .The UAE: Heritage and History," Official Website of Tourism in the United Arab Emirates.
80-" .Islamic Civilization in the UAE: Heritage and History," Emirates Culture Center, 2020.
81-" .UAE Vision 2021: Prosperity and Sustainable Development," Official Website of the UAE Government.
82-" .Economic Development in the UAE: Strategies and Achievements," Ministry of Economic Planning and Development in the UAE.
83-" .Cultural and Social Development in the UAE: Challenges and Achievements," Emirates Center for Studies and Research.
84-" .UAE Vision 2071: Directives for the Future," Official Website of the UAE Government.

85-" .National Strategy for Education and Human Development," Ministry of Education and Knowledge Development in the UAE.

86-" .Burj Khalifa: Symbol of Architectural Innovation in the UAE," Official Burj Khalifa Website.

87-" .Dubai World Trade Center: Hub of Trade and Innovation in the UAE," Official Dubai World Website.

88-" .UAE Vision 2071: Sustainable Development Strategy," Official Website of the UAE Government.

89-" .UAE Strategy for Sustainable Development 2030," Ministry of Economic Development in the UAE.

90-" .Sustainable Development and Environment in the UAE: Challenges and Achievements," Official Website of the UAE Government.

91-" .Renewable Energy in the UAE: Vision and Achievements," UAE Energy Authority.

92-" .Education Strategy in the UAE," Ministry of Education and Knowledge Development in the UAE.

93-" .Cultural Innovation and Community Development in the UAE," Official Website of the UAE Government.

94-" .The UAE: Journey of Development and Progress," Ministry of Planning and Development in the UAE.

95-" .Sustainable Development and Environmental Protection in the UAE," Ministry of Climate Change and Environment in the UAE.

96-" .Higher Education in the UAE: Challenges and Opportunities," Report from the UAE University Council.

97-" .Economic Development Strategy in the UAE," Ministry of Planning and Development in the UAE.

98-" .Economic Development in the UAE: Challenges and Opportunities," National Center for Studies and Research in the UAE.

99-" .Innovation and Entrepreneurship in the UAE: Vision 2021," National Innovation Authority in the UAE.

100-" .UAE Innovation and Technology Strategy 2031," Ministry of Culture and Knowledge Development in the UAE.

101-" .UAE Vision for Digital Economy and Innovation," UAE Economic Development Council.

102-" .National Strategy for Green Technology and Sustainable Economy," Ministry of Climate Change in the UAE.

103-" .State of the Environment Report in the UAE," Environment and Energy Authority in the UAE.

104-" .Sustainable Development Plan 2021-2031," National Economic Development Council in the UAE.

105-" .Sustainable Infrastructure Strategy for the UAE," Ministry of Public Works in the UAE.

106- .Official Portal of the United Arab Emirates Government.

107- .Federal Authority for Information Technology and Telecommunications - [link].

108- .Ministry of Human Resources and Emiratisation - [link].

109- .International Conference on e-Government - [link].

110-" .Smart Leadership: Towards a Bright Future" - Book by Sheikh Mohammed bin Rashid Al Maktoum.

111-" .The UAE: Past, Present, and Future" - Ibrahim Al Abiad, Dar Al Adab.

112-" .Impact of Geographic Environment on Civilizations' Development" - Mohammed Al Khudairy, Geography and Development Magazine.

113-" .Social Transformations in the UAE" - Abdullah Al Balushi, Social and Humanitarian Research Magazine.

114- .Women Empowerment Strategy - Official Portal of the United Arab Emirates Government.

115-" .UAE Vision 2021," available at: https://vision2021.ae/ar

116-" .UAE Vision 2031," available at: https://www.vision2030.ae/ar

117-" .Digital Competitiveness Index 2020," available at: https://www.oxfordinsights.com/dci-2020

118-" .Digital UAE | Official Portal of the United Arab Emirates Government (u.ae)

" .119-Personal Data Protection Law in the UAE," National Cybersecurity Authority.

120-" .Global Competitiveness Report 2023," World Economic Forum.

121-" .UAE Government's Digital Strategy - 2025 | Official Portal of the United Arab Emirates Government (u.ae)

122-" .UAE Strategy for Digital Infrastructure Development," Ministry of Infrastructure and Urban Development.

123-" .Cyber Safety and Digital Security | Official Portal of the United Arab Emirates Government (u.ae)

124-" .Information Security Assurance System in the UAE | Official Portal of the United Arab Emirates Government (u.ae)

125-" .Cybersecurity and Safety | Official Portal of the United Arab Emirates Government (u.ae)

126-" .Cybersecurity Council | Official Portal of the United Arab Emirates Government (u.ae)

127-" .Digital Transformation | Official Portal of the United Arab Emirates Government (u.ae)

128-" .UAE Government's Digital Strategy - 2025 | Official Portal of the United Arab Emirates Government (u.ae)

130-" .Facts and Figures about Digital Transformation | Official Portal of the United Arab Emirates Government (u.ae)

131-" .Cybersecurity and Safety | Official Portal of the United Arab Emirates Government (u.ae)

132-" .Facts and Figures about Digital Transformation | Official Portal of the United Arab Emirates Government (u.ae)

133-" .UAE Government's Digital Strategy - 2025 | Official Portal of the United Arab Emirates Government (u.ae)

134- .Telecommunications and Digital Government Regulatory Authority (tdra.gov.ae)

135-" .Human Development Report in Sharjah 2023," Sharjah Government.

136-" .General Authority for Statistics - Sharjah".

137-" .Official Website of the Sharjah Government".

138-" .Human Development Report in Ras Al Khaimah," Ras Al Khaimah Government.

139-" .Statistics Authority - Ras Al Khaimah".

140-" .Official Website of the Ras Al Khaimah Government".

141-" .Sustainable Development Report in the UAE," National Energy Management Authority.

142-" .UAE and the Vision 2030 for Sustainable Development," Emirates News Agency.

143-Ministry of Climate Change and Environment Website - UAE".

144-" .National Energy Strategy for the UAE," Ministry of Energy and Infrastructure.

145-" .Environmental Sustainability in the UAE - Status Report," Ministry of Climate Change and Environment.

146-" .Sustainable Development Report for the UAE 2025," Environment Agency - Abu Dhabi.

147-" .Urban Transportation Strategy in the UAE," Ministry of Infrastructure.

148-" .Official Website of the Ministry of Infrastructure - UAE".

149-" .UAE Vision 2021." UAE eGovernment Portal.

150-" .Government and Political System | Official Portal of the United Arab Emirates Government (u.ae)

151-" .The United Arab Emirates: Power and Role Transformations | Al Jazeera Center for Studies (aljazeera.net)

152-" .Emirati Diplomacy: Strategic Relations with the World | Gulf Newspaper (alkhaleej.ae)

153-" .The UAE's Rich Record in Promoting Peace and Stability Worldwide (mofa.gov.ae)

154-" .The Future Outlook of UAE Society" - Professor Dr. Jamal Saeed Al Suwaidi

155-Vision 2021: UAE National Agenda", Government of UAE.

156-UAE Vision 2071", Ministry of Cabinet Affairs and the Future.

157-The UAE's Vision for Sustainable Development", Emirates News Agency.

158-Al Mubarak, M. (2018). "Reflections on the UAE's Cultural Renaissance." The Emirates Review, 12(3), 45-52.

159-Al-Kaabi, M. (2020). "The Role of Education in the Cultural Renaissance of the UAE." Journal of Educational and Psychological Studies, 14(2), 78-91.

160-Gulf News. (2022). "UAE Cultural Renaissance: A Journey Towards Modernity."

161-Smith, J. (2021). "The Economic Renaissance of the UAE: Strategies and Success Factors." Journal of Economic Development, 25(2), 67-82.

162-Al-Falasi, M. (2019). "Education and Human Development in the UAE: Challenges and Opportunities." International Journal of Educational Development, 15(3), 112-125.

163-Emirates News Agency. (2022). "UAE's Vision for the Future: A Journey of Success and Achievement."

164-Al-Marzouqi, F. (2019). "Leadership Vision and Sustainable Development: The Case of the UAE." Journal of Sustainable Development Studies, 6(2), 45-58.

165-Emirates News Agency. (2022). "Leadership Vision: A Driving Force for Sustainable Development."

166-The UAE's Path to Modernity: The Story of a Nation's Renaissance ،" مقالة في مجلةGulf News.

167-The United Arab Emirates: A Modern History بقلم "Mohammad Al Fahim.

168-From Pearls to Oil: How the Oil Industry Shaped the United Arab Emirates ،"The National.

169-From Vision to Reality: The UAE's Journey of Development", UAE Ministry of Cabinet Affairs and the Future.

170-Vision 2021: UAE National Agenda", Government of UAE.

171-UAE Vision 2071", Ministry of Cabinet Affairs and the Future.

172-The UAE's Commitment to Gender Equality," Emirates News Agency, WAM.(2022)

173-Women in the UAE: Challenges and Opportunities," Ministry of Community Development, UAE.(2023)

174-Education and Women's Empowerment in the UAE," UAE Ministry of Education.(2021)

175-Empowering Women in the UAE: Success Stories," Emirates Women's Union.(2020)

176-Women in Leadership: A Case Study of the UAE," Dubai School of Government Research Paper Series.(2019)

177-United Nations E-Government Survey 2020.

178-World Bank Group, "E-Government Development Index."

179-UAE Vision 2021" - Government of the United Arab Emirates.

180-The Role of Visionary Leadership in Urban Development" - UAE Ministry of Infrastructure Development.

182-Sustainable Infrastructure Development in the UAE" - UAE National Agenda.

183-Investment in Infrastructure in the UAE" - UAE Ministry of Infrastructure Development.

184-UAE National Agenda for Infrastructure Development" - UAE National Bureau of Statistics.

185-Economic Impact of Government Investments in Infrastructure" - UAE Ministry of Economy.

186-Vision 2021 - National Agenda." UAE Government Portal, www.government.ae/en/about-the-uae/vision-2021-national-agenda.

187-UAE's Education Vision." UAE Ministry of Education, www.moe.gov.ae/en/about-the-ministry/Pages/educationVision.aspx.

188-Higher Education in the UAE." UAE Embassy, www.uae-embassy.org/discover-uae/education/higher-education-uae.

189-Ministry of Health and Prevention UAE. "Healthcare System inUAE."[MoHAP](https://www.mohap.gov.ae/en/services/Pages/healthCareSystem.aspx).

190-Alameri, Hamad Saeed. "The Future of Healthcare in the United Arab Emirates: Innovation and Digital Transformation." Journal of the Saudi Heart Association, vol. 33, no. 4, 2021, pp. 557-563.

191-Ministry of Education UAE. "Research and Innovation in the UAE."[MoE](https://www.moe.gov.ae/en/AboutTheMinistry/Pages/ResearchAndInnovation.aspx).

192-UAE National Research Foundation. "Research Strategy 2021-2031." [NRF](https://www.nrf.ae/research-strategy-2021-2031/).

193-UAE Gender Balance Council. "Empowering Women in the UAE." [Gender Balance Council] (https://www.gbc.gov.ae/).

194-Ministry of Youth UAE. "Youth Empowerment Initiatives." [MoY](https://www.youth.gov.ae/en/Initiatives)

195-UAE Ministry of Economy. "Economic Diversification in the UAE." [MoE](https://www.economy.gov.ae/en/about-the-ministry/strategies-and-plans/economic-diversification).

196-UAE Ministry of Education. "Education in the UAE." [MoE](https://www.moe.gov.ae/en/AboutTheMinistry/Pages/default.aspx).

446-Al-Falasi, Hessa. "Social Development in the UAE: Achievements and Challenges." Emirates Social Development Council, vol. 8, no. 2, 2023, pp. 45-58

197-Al Mubarak, Mohamed Khalifa. "Contemporary Architecture in the UAE: Balancing Modernity and Heritage." UAE Ministry of Culture and Youth, 2022.

198-Al-Shehhi, Fatima. "Preserving Cultural Heritage in the UAE: Challenges and Opportunities." Emirates

199-Heritage Association, vol. 12, no. 3, 2023, pp. 78-91.

200-Abu Dhabi's Journey From a Bedouin Town to a Global Metropolis" - The National.

201-Abu Dhabi's Evolution as a Cultural Capital" - Abu Dhabi Culture.

202-The Rise of Urban Development in the UAE" - Gulf News.

203-Strategies for Economic Growth in Sharjah, Ajman, and Ras Al Khaimah" - The National.

204-The Sharjah Urban Renaissance" - Sharjah Government Portal.

205-Sharjah: A Hub of Culture and Innovation" - Visit Sharjah.

206-Ajman City Guide - Discovering the Emirate's Architectural Identity." UAE Interact, www.uaeinteract.com/travel/ajman.asp.

207-Ajman's Ambitious Growth Plans and Smart City Vision." Zawya,www.zawya.com/mena/en/business/story/Ajmans_ambitious_growth_plans_and_smart_city_vision-SNG_161882962/.

208-Ajman Vision 2021: Designing a City That Promotes Connectivity and Convenience." ME Construction News, www.constructionweekonline.com/article-48692-ajman-vision-2021-designing-a-city-that-promotes-connectivity-and-convenience

209-Ministry of Cabinet Affairs and the Future. "UAE Vision 2021." [MCAF](https://www.vision2021.ae/).

210-UAE Ministry of Economy. "National Agenda: Key Performance Indicators."[MoE](https://www.economy.gov.ae/en/strategy-and-the-future/national-agenda).

211-UAE Ministry of Foreign Affairs and International Cooperation. "Foreign Policy of the UAE: Priorities and
Objectives."[MoFAIC](https://www.mofaic.gov.ae/en/home.aspx).

212-Al-Hamadi, Khalid. "The Role of the UAE in Regional Diplomacy: Achievements and

213-Challenges." Emirates Diplomatic Journal, vol. 10, no. 2, 2023, pp. 55-68

214-UAE Ministry of Foreign Affairs and International Cooperation. "UAE's International Partnerships."
[MoFAIC](https://www.mofaic.gov.ae/en/home.aspx).

215-Emirates Red Crescent. "Humanitarian Initiatives by the UAE."
[ERC](https://www.rcuae.ae/).

216-UAE Ministry of Climate Change and Environment. "Environmental Initiatives and Partnerships."
[MoCCAE](https://www.moccae.gov.ae/en/home.aspx)

217-UAE Ministry of Foreign Affairs and International Cooperation. "UAE's Contributions to Global Peace and Development." MoFAIC.

218-UAE Ministry of International Cooperation and Development. "UAE's Humanitarian Aid and Development Initiatives." MoICD.

219-UAE Ministry of Climate Change and Environment. "UAE's Environmental Initiatives and Sustainable Development Efforts." MoCCAE.

220-UAE Ministry of Economy. "National Innovation Strategy."
[MoE](https://www.economy.gov.ae/en/strategy-and-the-future/national-innovation-strategy).

221-UAE National Media Council. "UAE's Cultural Diplomacy Initiatives."
[NMC](https://www.nmc.gov.ae/en-us/home.aspx).

222-UAE Ministry of Climate Change and Environment. "Sustainability and Environmental Initiatives."
[MoCCAE](https://www.moccae.gov.ae/en/home.aspx).

223-The UAE Economy: Past, Present, and Future" - Ministry of Economy, UAE.

224-Population Growth and Urban Development in the UAE" - UAE National Bureau of Statistics.

225-The Impact of Economic Diversification on Infrastructure Development in the UAE" - UAE Ministry of Infrastructure Development.

226-UAE Ministry of Foreign Affairs and International Cooperation. "UAE's International Partnerships." MoFAIC.

227-Emirates Red Crescent. "Humanitarian Initiatives by the UAE." ERC.

228-UAE Ministry of Climate Change and Environment. "Environmental Initiatives and Partnerships." MoCCAE.